Contents

Unit 1: Serious Plays

Bill Tuttle is a good truck driver, but he has one limitation. He cannot read. Realizing the problem, a group of teens convinces a community center to offer reading classes for adults. At first reluctant, Bill finally agrees to attend.
(10 characters, reading levels 2.0 to 5.9)

Jimmy Valentine, a reformed safecracker, pulls one last job—even though it might mean his return to prison. Adapted from an O. Henry short story.
(10 characters, reading levels 2.0 to 5.6)

Kevin Jackson, upset by his parents' separation, destroys a Christmas display. Kevin is ashamed of what he has done, and with the help of Mr. Walker, a teacher, Kevin learns how to "turn something hurting into something positive."
(9 characters, reading levels 2.0 to 5.3)

Juan Villa feels like an outcast because of his disability until he meets Annie, a woman with a hearing disability. She gives him the inspiration to succeed despite his personal problems.
(10 characters, reading levels 2.0 to 5.0)

Unit 2: Humorous Plays

Teenage fans concoct a plan to sneak backstage at a Lance Britney concert, only to discover that their idol is not who they thought he was.
(8 characters, reading levels 2.0 to 6.0)

In a comedy of errors, most everyone in Clone City gets cloned by a mad scientist. One private eye figures it out, only to find himself face-to-face with his own clone.
(13 characters, reading levels 2.0 to 6.0)

Many famous folktale and tall-tale characters gather for a "showdown" to prove who is the biggest folk hero of all.
(9 characters, reading levels 2.5 to 5.5)

Extension Activities for Plays

Unit 3: Poems for Choral Reading

Introduction

★ Overview

Readers' Theater II is a supplemental reading program designed to increase students' vocabulary, comprehension, and fluency. This collection of seven high-interest plays will draw in even the most reluctant readers and help build their self-confidence through oral reading. The selections include both serious plays and humorous plays. Also included are several poems divided in parts for choral reading.

The National Reading Panel has identified fluency as one of the five basic areas of reading instruction. Readers' theater is recognized as a significant instructional method to improve fluency.

The National Council of Teachers of English proclaimed in a resolution requesting funding for workshops and experimental theater companies "that live performances are the most effective way to help students comprehend and appreciate dramatic literature." Giving students the opportunity to participate in *Readers' Theater II* is a fitting introduction to the pleasures of drama.

★ A Variety of Reading Levels

Almost every student will be able to participate comfortably because of the wide range of reading levels found in the plays. Each play has eight to thirteen characters. Reading levels for individual characters range from 2.0 to 6.0 as measured by the Spache and Dale-Chall readability formulas.

★ The Teacher's Guide

The two-page Teacher's Guide before each play provides easy-to-follow teaching suggestions for that play.

Meet the Players provides a list of characters and identifies the readability levels for each part. The list may be used to assign appropriate parts based on students' reading levels. You may wish to read the most difficult part when necessary. In small groups, you may wish to assign one character's part to several students.

Play Summary provides an overview of each play. You may use the summary to become familiar with the plot of the play quickly.

Vocabulary lists most words in the play that are at or above the sixth-grade level. In some cases, words may be familiar, but their usage within the context of the play may not. According to current research, familiarity with vocabulary is a prerequisite for fluency. Therefore, emphasize these words in vocabulary exercises before students read a play. English language learners may need special attention from teachers.

Tapping Prior Knowledge prepares and motivates students to read the play. Several questions are provided that elicit personal responses from students—based on individual experiences and feelings.

Thinking It Over provides questions that can be used after students have read a play. The questions can be used to monitor students' comprehension of the play.

Presenting the Play suggests the sound effects and props needed to present the play as a radio play or a classroom play.

Extending the Play provides ideas for cross-curricular activities, including language arts, social studies, and writing. The activities may be used to enrich the students' reading of the play in individual, small, and large groups.

Comprehension Activities

Four comprehension activities follow each play.

What Do You Remember? indicates the students' understanding of facts, sequence, and context in the play. Questions about main idea, conclusion, and inference are also included. A short-answer writing question concludes this page.

What's That Word? is a vocabulary enrichment page. A variety of exercises reinforces the higher-level vocabulary words in each play.

What Do You Think? allows students to explore some of the concepts presented in the play. Activities involve students in drawing and thinking about the content of the play.

Write Away! requires students to combine a readers' theater experience with composition skills. The exercises are designed to elicit both analytical and creative responses to the ideas explored in the plays.

 ## *Extension Activities*

The extension activities on pages 164–168 may be reproduced for use in the classroom or at home. Any or all of the five activity masters can be used after completion of a play. You may wish to assign different activities to individual students based on their abilities. You may also wish to have students work cooperatively in pairs or in groups to complete the activities.

Studying the Elements of a Play asks students to complete sentences describing a play's characters, setting, and plot.

Comparing Characters is a chart students use to describe two characters' personality traits. Students then write a paragraph comparing the two characters.

Understanding the Characters encourages students to describe characters based on their dialogue and actions.

Making a Play Map is a means by which students track the events in a play.

Choosing an Alternate Ending challenges students to write a new ending for a play.

 ## *Choral Reading*

In choral reading, students read an assigned part, usually in unison. A few selections feature solo parts for dramatic emphasis. As the selection is read, students practice word recognition, expand reading vocabulary, and increase comprehension skills. Choral reading experiences build readers' confidence by organizing them into a community of readers. Readers build fluency with texts that feature elements such as rhyme, rhythm, and repetition—perfect for oral reading.

CONGRATULATIONS!

Let all know that

_____

is a Super Reader!

This reader's favorite selection is

_____

By the Book

Meet the Players

Character	Reading Level
Narrator	5.9
Bill Tuttle, *a truck driver*	4.6
Pedro Garcia, *Bill's boss*	2.0
Sam Murphy, *Bill's co-worker*	2.0
Tommy Chan, *Bill's friend*	4.7
Rowena Simpson, *Bill's friend*	2.1
Marie Brown, *Bill's friend*	5.2
First Woman, *apartment resident*	2.0
Second Woman, *apartment resident*	2.0
Olna Green, *community center director*	3.0

Play Summary

Bill Tuttle is a good truck driver, but he has one severe limitation. He cannot read. He relies on his ability to memorize and the help of three teenagers—Tommy, Rowena, and Marie—he has befriended to read and organize his deliveries. Realizing Bill's limitation, the teenagers convince some older community members to start reading classes for adults. At first Bill is reluctant to attend the classes because he is ashamed to admit to anyone that he cannot read. However, when he learns a co-worker cannot read either, he decides to attend the classes.

Vocabulary

supervising, p. 9   *bluff*, p. 13   *absolute*, p. 20
ramp, pp. 9, 10   *exasperation*, p. 14 *constantly*, p. 23
awesome, p. 11   *elementary*, p. 15   *literacy*, p. 24
scowls, p. 13   *admit*, p. 17   *dedicated*, p. 24

Tapping Prior Knowledge

Before reading the play, discuss these questions with students.

1. In what ways would your life be affected if you could not read?

2. What is the best reason you can think of for learning how to read?

3. If you knew a friend could not read, what would you do? Explain your answer.

By the Book

Thinking It Over

The following questions may be used for oral discussion or as written exercises.

1. Even though he couldn't read, Bill Tuttle managed to make his deliveries every day. How did he do that?
2. When Tommy, Rowena, and Marie helped Bill organize his deliveries, were they really helping him? Explain why or why not.
3. What reasons did Bill give for never having learned how to read? What reasons did he give for not wanting to attend adult classes? Do you think he had good reasons, or was he just making excuses? Explain your answer.
4. Why did Bill finally agree to attend reading classes?

Presenting the Play

Radio Play: Use these sound effects to present *By the Book* as a radio play.

- taped music to indicate act breaks—pp. 12, 16, 19, 20, 22, 24
- truck starting up and driving away—Act One, pp. 10, 12; Act Six, p. 23
- truck stopping and truck door opening/shutting—Act One, p. 10; Act Five, p. 21; Act Six, p. 23
- knock on door—Act Two, pp. 13–16
- door slamming—Act Two, pp. 14, 16
- applause—Act Seven, p. 24

Classroom Play: To stage the play in the classroom, use the sound effects listed for the radio play and the props listed below.

- delivery list—Act One, p. 9; Act Two, p. 12; Act Five, pp. 21, 22; Act Six, p. 23
- boxes and packages for delivery—Act One, pp. 9–11; Act Two, pp. 12–16
- chairs arranged as cab of truck—Act One, pp. 10, 12; Act Two, p. 12; Act Five, p. 21; Act Six, p. 23
- stickball equipment—Act One, p. 10
- nameplates for apartment doors—Act Two, pp. 12–16
- desk and chairs for office—Act Three, pp. 18–19; Act Four, p. 20

Teacher Notes

Extending the Play

Use these activities to enrich the students' experience with readers' theater.

1. Use any or all of the blackline masters on pages 164–168.
2. Have students draw or paint a mural illustrating a number of jobs in which the ability to read is critical for success.
3. Tell students to write an editorial for their local newspaper to try to convince community members that adult literacy is important.

READERS' THEATER II

Presents

By the Book

by
Peggy Warner

SVR 2B8

Cast

(in order of appearance)

Narrator

Bill Tuttle, *a truck driver*

Pedro García, *Bill's boss*

Sam Murphy, *a worker on the loading dock*

Tommy Chan, *Bill's friend*

Rowena Simpson, *Bill's friend*

Marie Brown, *Bill's friend*

First Woman, *a resident at 34 Green Street*

Second Woman, *a resident at 34 Green Street*

Olna Green, *director of the Martin Luther King, Jr., Center*

Act One

Narrator: Bill Tuttle has a new job. He's been working as a driver for the Ace Trucking Company for two weeks. Each day he reports to work and picks up the list of deliveries he has to make. Since he loves to drive, Bill thinks he has the perfect job. And he does, except for one big problem.

Bill: What's in for me today, Mr. Garcia?

Pedro: You've got seven drops. They're all right here around Gastonia.

Bill: *(Stuffing the list into his shirt pocket)* That sounds good to me. See you at the end of the day.

Pedro: Aren't you even going to look at where you're going?

Bill: I always do that when I'm in the cab.

Pedro: Okay, Bill, you have a good day. Drive carefully.

Bill: I always do, Mr. Garcia. *(Glancing at his watch)* It's time to check with Sam to see if we're all set to go.

Narrator: Bill walks over to the loading ramp where Sam Murphy is supervising the loading of several large trucks.

Sam: You're all set, Bill. I had the office machine put in the last box. I figured you might want to drop that off first.

Bill: You're right, Sam. That makes sense.

Narrator: Bill gets into the truck and backs it out of the loading ramp. Smiling and waving to Sam Murphy, he turns onto the street. That's when Bill's smile vanishes. He drives for several blocks, peering out the window, as if he's looking for something or someone.

Bill: *(Talking to himself)* Sure hope those kids are playing ball today. Otherwise, I'll have to . . . *(Smiling in relief)* There they are!

Narrator: Bill pulls his truck over to the curb. He gets out and strolls over to a group of teenagers playing stickball in an empty lot.

Bill: Hey, kids, how are you doing today?

Teenagers: *(Together)* Hi, Mr. Tuttle!

Marie: Want to play a little stickball, Mr. Tuttle?

Bill: Thanks, Marie, but I don't have time.

Tommy: You want us to help with your deliveries again?

Bill: *(Taking the list from his shirt pocket)* Yes, that's right.

Narrator: The teenagers gather around as Bill unfolds his delivery list.

Tommy: First one's easy. It says J. Kopesky at 34 Green Street.

Rowena: You're supposed to drop off just one package there.

Bill: Okay. Kopesky. Green Street. A package. Got it. The second one is for A & A, right? They're on First Street.

Marie: That's right, Mr. Tuttle. See, you can read!

Bill: *(Blushing)* Not really, Marie. I just recognized the letter A, and I've been there before. It's the names that have a lot of letters that give me trouble. Now, what's next?

Narrator: With the teenagers' help, Bill goes through his entire list. The teenagers go to Bill's truck and put all the packages in the right order according to the list. Then Bill repeats the name of each person or company receiving the package, the street, and what has to be dropped off.

Tommy: You sure have some awesome memory, Mr. Tuttle!

Bill: That's because I use it a lot, Tommy. A memory can be a lot like playing stickball. If you don't practice often, you sort of lose your edge. Know what I mean?

Marie: I guess that makes sense. But if you have such a good memory, Mr. Tuttle, how come you never learned to read?

Bill: The letters got all mixed up on me. Then I kind of fooled around instead of paying attention. I . . . I never did graduate from high school.

Tommy: So, why don't you go back to school?

Bill: *(Laughing)* I'm afraid I'm a bit too old for that, Tommy. Besides, I've already got a good job. I don't have time anymore. And speaking of time, I'd better get moving.

Narrator: The teenagers wave as Bill drives away.

Rowena: Poor Mr. Tuttle.

Tommy: It must be tough. Not being able to read, I mean. Sure wish there was something we could do to help him.

Act Two

Narrator: Bill drives to the first address on his delivery list. Number 34 Green Street is an apartment building. But when Bill opens the front door and steps into the hall, he knows he is in trouble.

Bill: Oh, no. There's two doors and two nameplates here. Which one of them is J. Kopesky's?

Narrator: Bill scowls at the nameplate by the door on the right. One word is printed on it, but none of the letters look quite like a J. He crosses the hall. This nameplate is written in a very curly kind of lettering.

Bill: It might as well be worm tracks! I guess I'll just have to bluff this one.

Narrator: There is nothing Bill hates more than to look like a fool. And if anyone ever finds out he can't read—will he ever look foolish! He stands there and thinks.

Bill: I know!

Narrator: Moving very quietly, Bill slips the two nameplates out of their brass slots. Then he swaps the two. Now, the door on the right has the wrong name next to it, and so does the door on the left.

Bill: Well, here we go. *(Knocking on the door on the right)*

Narrator: A very well-dressed woman comes to the door.

Bill: *(Brightly)* Delivery for J. Kopesky!

First Woman: *(Staring coldly at Bill)* Oh, really? Do I look like a J. Kopesky, young man? If you'd take the time to read my nameplate, you'd see that it plainly says Carolyn Weatherby.

Narrator: She pronounces her own name as if it is a very special name indeed.

Bill: *(Turning to stare at her nameplate)* Funny, that's not what it says.

First Woman: *(With exasperation)* Oh, really! *(Leaning out the door so she, too, can read the nameplate)* Oh! How very odd. That's not my nameplate.

Bill: *(Cheerfully)* Sure you're in the right apartment, then?

Narrator: The woman gives a little jump, as if the thought startles her. Then she glares at Bill and slams the door.

Bill: Well, I didn't make any points there! But at least now I know that if she isn't J. Kopesky, then the door on the left must be Kopesky's.

Narrator: So he knocks on the door on the left, and someone inside asks him what he wants.

Bill: Delivery for J. Kopesky!

Narrator: The voice yells back that Joe Kopesky lives upstairs.

Bill: Oh, no! *(Looking farther down the hall)* I didn't even see that elevator. At least I've learned one thing now. J. Kopesky is a guy.

Narrator: So Bill takes the elevator to the second floor. There are three doors in this hallway, each with a nameplate to the right of the door.

Bill: Gosh, I'm losing time here! I've got to solve this quickly.

Narrator: Bill knocks on the door on the right, but no one answers. He knocks on the middle door. A young woman opens the door and smiles at him.

Second Woman: May I help you?

Bill: *(Pointing to the door on the right)* Can you tell me when your neighbor will be back, Miss?

Second Woman: I'm sorry, but Mr. Jones is gone for the day. *(Closing the door)* Perhaps you can try him after five.

Bill: Well, now I've learned that Kopesky doesn't live behind the door on the right. And I know that a woman lives behind the middle door. Therefore, it's elementary, my dear Watson. The mysterious J. Kopesky lives here! *(Knocking loudly on the door on the left)*

Narrator: No one answers the door. But Bill can hear music coming from inside the apartment, so he knocks again.

Bill: *(Still sure of his reasoning)* Mr. Kopesky! I've got a package for you.

Narrator: A man comes to the door and tells Bill that Kopesky and his wife live next door. The man nods at the middle door, slams his own door, and goes back inside. Bill's ears are very red.

Bill: Why didn't I think of that? *(Sighing)* Guess she didn't look old enough to be married, that's why. I figured she lived alone. *(Knocking on the middle door again)*

Narrator: The same woman comes to the door again and seems surprised to see Bill.

Bill: Mrs. Kopesky? Turns out I have a package for you, too. That is, I have a package for your husband. Could you sign here, please?

Second Woman: *(Signing for the package)* My husband will be so pleased! Do you also have a package for my next-door neighbor, Mr. Jones? I can keep it here for him if you like.

Bill: Oh! *(Thinking fast)* Oh, no, but would you tell him that . . . that . . . Henry . . . Bill Henry stopped by. And tell him I said hello.

Narrator: Bill hurries away. The woman stands there and stares after him.

Bill: *(To himself)* Gosh, what a mess! And now poor Jones is going to be wondering who Bill Henry is and why he would visit him. Oh, well, I can't worry about it now.

End of Act Two

Act Three

Narrator: While Bill Tuttle is having his problems across town, Tommy and his friends are sitting on Marie's porch.

Tommy: I've been thinking. When my grandmother came from China to live with us, it took her a long time to learn to speak English. She still can't read it.

Marie: What does that have to do with Mr. Tuttle?

Tommy: I bet lots of people like my grandmother and Mr. Tuttle never learned to read. They're too ashamed to admit it. So, they get other people to read for them.

Rowena: Like Mr. Tuttle gets us to read for him?

Tommy: Right. Mr. Tuttle thinks we're helping him. But we're not really. We're just keeping him from learning how to read for himself.

Marie: Wait a minute, Tommy. Are you saying we should stop helping Mr. Tuttle so he'll be forced to learn?

Tommy: No, he'd only find someone else to read for him. But did you see the news last night? They started reading classes for adults over in Middletown. I bet we could get one of those going here in Gastonia.

Rowena: That's a great idea, Tommy! But how could we do that? I mean, we can't teach adults.

Tommy: What if we tried to get some adults to teach?

Marie: *(Excitedly)* I know where we can try—the Martin Luther King, Jr., Center! They do all kinds of stuff for people who live around here.

Tommy: It's worth a try. Come on. Let's go!

Narrator: It takes the teenagers only a few minutes to reach the center. A smiling woman greets them at the front desk.

Olna: Hello, I'm Mrs. Olna Green—the director of the Martin Luther King, Jr., Center. May I be of any assistance to you today?

Narrator: The teenagers introduce themselves.
Then . . .

Tommy: Well, you see, there's this man.

Rowena: And he drives a truck.

Marie: And he can't read.

Olna: *(Laughing)* Wait! Slow down a bit and speak one at a time, please. Tommy, since you started things, why not finish the story?

Narrator: Tommy tells Mrs. Green about Bill Tuttle and their idea.

Tommy: So, we thought it would be great if you started a reading class here at the King Center. The center helps people in the community, right? You have programs for adults like our friend and my grandmother.

Olna: Yes, we offer things like free breakfasts and finding housing, and we can occasionally help find jobs. But I'm afraid I can't assist you right now because we just don't have the money to start up a reading program—not this year, anyway. Our budget's been cut and—well, maybe next year we'll be able to.

Narrator: Quite disappointed by Olna Green's answer, the teenagers leave in silence.

Act Four

Narrator: The next morning, the teenagers meet in the empty lot.

Tommy: I'm sure our idea would work. And I've been thinking about how we can do it. Mrs. Green said the center doesn't have any money, right? Well, what if we set the program up ourselves? If we got people to volunteer as teachers, then all we'd need from her is a room at the center to hold the classes in.

Marie: Good thinking, Tommy! *(Pauses)* My mom's real smart. She'll help, I'm sure.

Rowena: My brother's studying to be a teacher. I know he'll help this summer if I ask him. But what about books?

Tommy: We'll ask the library to donate some—or maybe lend them!

Marie: Tommy, you're an absolute genius!

Tommy: *(Blushing)* Not quite. We still have to convince Mrs. Green to go along.

Narrator: Again the teenagers troop down to the center. This time, convincing Mrs. Green is a lot easier than they expect.

Olna: Well, now, you might have something after all. If you can round up enough teachers and if you prove you can get the books, why, I bet I'll be able to convince our board of directors we should provide the space. I think I can also find a little money to help you advertise for students.

Tommy: Mrs. Green, that would be great! We'll be back as soon as we can!

End of Act Four

Act Five

Narrator: The teenagers are excited about the things that have to be done. They meet in the empty lot the next morning to talk about their progress.

Rowena: My brother says he'll be glad to help.

Marie: My mom will help, too. She's even getting a few other friends to help with the teaching.

Tommy: That's good news! Mr. Ortega at the library said they had a ton of books they could give us. They're old, he said, but still good. I guess I was only half successful, though. *(Pauses)* My grandmother is something else. I think she wants to come to class, but she's afraid.

Marie: I sure hope Mr. Tuttle will join.

Rowena: *(Looking towards the street)* Speaking of Mr. Tuttle . . .

Bill: *(Walking over to the teenagers)* Morning, kids. Can you give me a hand with my list?

Tommy: Of course, Mr. Tuttle. But what's going to happen when school starts? We won't be around in the morning then.

Bill: *(Shrugging his shoulders)* I guess I'll have to find someone else. It won't be easy, though. A lot of people laugh when they find out I can't read. It's real embarrassing.

Rowena: Mr. Tuttle, what if there was a reading class you could go to? It wouldn't be a real school but a class where you'd be in with other adults who can't read, either.

Bill: My school days are over. You know my job keeps me busy all day.

Tommy: But there are lots of people like you, right here in Gastonia. People who never did learn to read for one reason or another. What if this place I'm thinking of would be open in the evening after work?

Bill: People like me, huh? I thought I was the only one around here who couldn't read.

Tommy: That's not so. Why, my grandmother can't read, either. And she's 70 years old!

Bill: Well, I'm still not sure something like that is for me, though. I never did like school.

Rowena: Won't you even try one class, Mr. Tuttle?

Marie: Oh, please, Mr. Tuttle? Try one class. You might like it!

Bill: *(Annoyed)* Look, kids, I like you. I really do. And I appreciate the help you give me. But don't push me. I'll handle my own problems in my own way, okay?

Narrator: Bill turns on his heel and goes to his truck. The list of deliveries is dangling from his hand, forgotten for the moment.

Tommy: Now we've done it. Here we try to help, and all we do is get Mr. Tuttle mad at us.

End of Act Five

Act Six

Narrator: Once in the truck, Bill realizes he has no idea where he is supposed to go. After driving around Gastonia for half an hour, constantly mumbling to himself, he suddenly drives back to the Ace Trucking Company. Ten minutes later he is standing with Sam Murphy at the loading dock.

Sam: Bill, what are you doing back here? It's not even noon. You can't have taken care of your deliveries.

Bill: Well, you're right, Sam. The thing is . . . I need some help. *(Shoving his list in Sam's face)* Read this for me, will you?

Sam: What's the problem, Bill? Did you forget your glasses?

Bill: Yes, Sam, that's it. I forgot my glasses.

Sam: Well, now, let's see. *(He moves the list closer to his eyes, then farther away.)* Let's see.

Bill: *(Impatiently)* What's wrong, Sam? Forget your glasses, too?

Sam: *(Embarrassed)* Bill, I . . . well . . . I guess you might as well know. You see, I can't read.

Bill: *(Shocked)* You can't read?

Sam: Well, no. That is . . . yes . . . I can't read.

Bill: *(Starting to laugh)* Sam Murphy, that's the funniest thing I've heard in my whole life!

Sam: *(Angrily)* What's so funny? If you only knew what it's like not to be able to . . .

Bill: *(Breaking in)* To read, Sam? I'll tell you why it's funny. I can't read either!

Sam: *(In disbelief)* You can't read either? Then how do you . . .

Bill: How do I make deliveries? That's a long story. Come on. We'll grab some coffee, and I'll tell you my secret. *(Pauses)* By the way, would you like to learn? To read, I mean.

Sam: Would I? Is Ace Trucking the best outfit in town?

Act Seven

Narrator: Discouraged as they are, Tommy and his two friends go ahead with their plans to organize an adult literacy class. Their hard work pays off, and Olna Green invites them to opening night exercises.

Olna: Without these three dedicated workers— Tommy Chan, Marie Brown, and Rowena Simpson—there would be no class. So let's give them a big round of applause, shall we?

Narrator: The students, 22 in all, including Tommy's grandmother, stand and applaud. Tommy, Marie, and Rowena move uneasily in their seats.

Olna: Well, I'm sure you are very anxious to begin learning. But first, *(Pauses)* kids, we have a little surprise for you. Will someone open the back door, please?

Narrator: A person in the back opens the door and stands aside to let two men enter.

Marie: *(Gasping)* Mr. Tuttle!

Bill: Right, Marie. And this is my friend, Sam Murphy.

Rowena: You're going to join the class!

Bill: *(Smiling)* I wouldn't miss it for the world.

Tommy: This is great! Gee, thanks, Mr. Tuttle!

Bill: I'm the one who should thank you, kids. And I will in a letter that I'll write myself. Why, I'll even read it to you over lunch at Joe's, just as soon as I complete the class!

End of Play

By the Book: What Do You Remember?

★ **Darken the letter by the correct answer.**

1. What is Bill Tuttle's job?
   Ⓐ school teacher
   Ⓑ center director
   Ⓒ truck driver
   Ⓓ ball player

2. When did Bill Tuttle decide to take the reading class?
   Ⓐ when the kids first asked him
   Ⓑ before the Kopesky delivery
   Ⓒ after he learned Sam Murphy could not read
   Ⓓ when Tommy's grandmother asked him

3. Bill Tuttle scowls when he cannot read the nameplates on the apartment doors. What does *scowls* mean?
   Ⓐ smiles
   Ⓑ makes an angry face
   Ⓒ whistles
   Ⓓ points

4. The play is mostly about how
   Ⓐ teenagers can be too nosy.
   Ⓑ community centers don't get enough money.
   Ⓒ delivery drivers don't need to know how to read.
   Ⓓ adults who cannot read are often embarrassed to admit it.

5. You can conclude that Bill Tuttle
   Ⓐ would lose his job as a driver.
   Ⓑ would go back to meet Mr. Jones.
   Ⓒ would learn how to read.
   Ⓓ would quit the reading class after one meeting.

6. The next time Bill Tuttle meets someone who cannot read, he will probably
   Ⓐ laugh at the person.
   Ⓑ tell the person to learn to read.
   Ⓒ tell the person to go away.
   Ⓓ send the person to see Mr. Jones.

7. How does Tommy associate his grandmother's experiences with Bill's problem?

   _____

   _____

   _____

By the Book: What's That Word?

 Use vocabulary words from the box to complete the puzzle.

| supervising |
| awesome |
| scowls |
| exasperation |
| elementary |
| admit |
| absolute |
| literacy |

Across

5. amazing

6. giving orders

7. to reveal or confess

8. the ability to read and write

Down

1. real, complete, or total

2. anger or annoyance

3. makes an angry face

4. simple or basic

By the Book: What Do You Think?

Many adults who cannot read are embarrassed to admit that fact. For whatever reason, they did not learn to read. Many of these adults would be willing to learn to read if they knew they would not face more embarrassment or exasperation.

★ Design a poster to attract adults to reading classes. Remember, the people who will see your poster cannot read.

✎ By the Book: Write Away!

Imagine that you are Bill Tuttle. Write a note thanking the teenagers for their help in setting up the reading classes. Tell them what you are doing now that you know how to read.

The Last Job

Meet the Players

Character	Reading Level
First Narrator	5.5
Second Narrator	5.6
Jimmy Valentine, *a safecracker*	4.5
Ben Price, *a detective*	3.2
Annabel Adams, *Jimmy Valentine's girlfriend*	2.4
Mr. Adams, *Annabel's father*	3.0
Jeanne Adams, *Annabel's sister*	2.1
Mike Dolan, *Jimmy Valentine's friend*	2.0
Prison Warden	2.7
Hotel Clerk	2.5

Play Summary

Jimmy Valentine, a safecracker, is pardoned by the governor but goes right back to a life of crime. After several burglaries, Jimmy moves, takes a new name, and opens a shoe store. Then he falls in love with Annabel Adams, daughter of the local banker. Jimmy is determined to mend his ways. But he uses his safecracking skills once again to save the life of Annabel's niece by freeing her from a locked bank vault. Jimmy is sure his new life will be destroyed by detective Ben Price. However, Ben is so impressed with Jimmy's selfless act that he decides to let Jimmy have his new life. Note: *The Last Job* is an adaptation of the short story "The Retrieved Reformation" by O. Henry (William Sydney Porter).

Vocabulary

pardon, p. 33

tasteful, p. 34

amalgamated, p. 34

tumblers, p. 35

resumed, p. 35

combination, pp. 35, 39

sociable, p. 36

captivated, p. 36

openings, p. 36

casually, p. 39

express, p. 39

economical, p. 39

convulsions, p. 40

presence, p. 40

unconscious, p. 40

Tapping Prior Knowledge

Before reading the play, discuss these questions with students.

1. Some stories and plays have happy endings, while others have sad ones. Which kind of ending do you like better? Explain your choice with an example from a story or play you have read recently.

2. Do you like surprise endings? Why or why not?

3. Can someone who has committed a crime change and live an honest life? Explain your answer.

The Last Job

Thinking It Over

The following questions may be used for oral discussion or as written exercises.

1. Why is *The Last Job* a good title for this play?

2. When did you first realize Jimmy was going back to cracking safes after his pardon? Point to a specific passage in the play to support your answer.

3. When Jimmy first saw Annabel Adams, we were told he "forgot who he was." What does that mean?

4. How did the play end? Were you satisfied with the ending? Explain why or why not.

Presenting the Play

Radio Play: Use these sound effects to present *The Last Job* as a radio play.

- taped music to indicate act breaks—pp. 33, 34, 36
- train stopping—Act Two, p. 34; Act Three, p. 35
- diners talking in cafe—Act Two, p. 34
- bank vault door slamming shut—Act Four, p. 39
- child screaming—Act Four, pp. 39, 40
- drill biting into metal—Act Four, p. 41
- bank vault door opening—Act Four, p. 41

Classroom Play: To stage the play in the classroom, use the sound effects listed for the radio play and the props listed below.

- five-dollar bill and railroad ticket—Act One, p. 33
- key—Act Two, p. 34
- collar button—Act Two, p. 35
- suitcase with burglar's tools—Act Two, pp. 34, 35; Act Three, p. 35; Act Four, pp. 39, 40
- newspaper—Act Three, p. 35
- desk and registry for hotel—Act Three, p. 36
- letter—Act Four, p. 37
- door for bank vault—Act Four, pp. 39–41
- drill—Act Four, p. 41

Extending the Play

Use these activities to enrich the students' experience with readers' theater.

1. Use any or all of the blackline masters on pages 164–168.

2. Have students write and illustrate a front-page newspaper report of Agatha's rescue.

3. Tell students to imagine they are Ben Price. Have them write a letter to Jimmy explaining why Ben did not arrest Jimmy when he had the chance.

4. Have students design a logo for Spencer's Shoe Store.

READERS' THEATER II

Presents

The Last Job

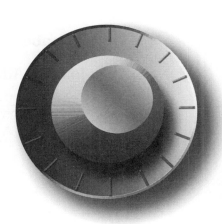

**Adaptation by Jack Warner
of an O. Henry short story**

Cast

(in order of appearance)

First Narrator

Second Narrator

Jimmy Valentine, *a safecracker*

Prison Warden

Mike Dolan, *Jimmy Valentine's friend*

Ben Price, *a detective*

Hotel Clerk

Annabel Adams, *Jimmy Valentine's girlfriend*

Jeanne Adams, *Annabel's sister*

Mr. Adams, *Annabel's father*

Act One

First Narrator: A guard goes to the prison shop where Jimmy Valentine is working and escorts him to the warden's office.

Second Narrator: There, the warden hands Jimmy his pardon, signed by the governor that morning.

Warden: Now, Valentine, you'll go out in the morning. Brace up and make a man of yourself. You're not a bad fellow at heart. Stop cracking safes and live an honest life.

Jimmy: Me, Warden? Why, I never cracked a safe in my life.

Warden: *(Chuckling)* Oh, no, of course you haven't. Let's see now. How was it you happened to be sent up on that Springfield job? Was it a case of a mean old jury that had it in for you?

Jimmy: Me? Why, Warden, I've never been in Springfield in my life.

Warden: *(To the prison guard)* Take him back to his cell, Cronin, and fix him up with outgoing clothes. Unlock him at seven in the morning and bring him to the release area. *(Turning to Jimmy)* Better think over my advice, Valentine.

First Narrator: At a quarter past seven the next morning, Jimmy stands in the warden's outer office. He is wearing a suit of ill-fitting clothes. The clerk gives him a five-dollar bill and a railroad ticket.

End of Act One

Act Two

Second Narrator: Three hours later, Jimmy steps off a train in a little town near the state line. He goes straight to the cafe of one Mike Dolan.

Mike: Feeling all right, Jimmy?

Jimmy: I'm just fine, Mike. Have you got my key?

Mike: I sure have, Jimmy. I've kept it here in the cash drawer all this time. *(Gets the key and hands it to Jimmy)*

First Narrator: Jimmy goes upstairs and unlocks the door of a room at the rear. Everything is just as he left it nearly ten months ago. There on the floor is Ben Price's collar button that was torn from the famous detective's shirt when Ben had overpowered Jimmy to arrest him. Pulling a folding bed out from the wall, Jimmy slides back a panel in the wall and drags out a dust-covered suitcase. He opens this and looks fondly at the finest set of burglar's tools in the East.

Second Narrator: A half hour later Jimmy goes downstairs and through the cafe. He is dressed in tasteful, well-fitting clothes and carries a dusted and cleaned suitcase in his hand.

Mike: Got any jobs lined up?

Jimmy: Me? I don't understand, Mike. I'm representing the New York Amalgamated Short Snap Biscuit Cracker and Frazzled Wheat Company.

Mike: *(Laughing loudly)* Oh, Jimmy, me boy. You'll never change, will you?

End of Act Two

Act Three

First Narrator: A week after the release of Jimmy Valentine, there is a neat safe job in Richmond, Indiana, with no clue to the author.

Second Narrator: Two weeks after that, a burglarproof safe in Logansport is robbed. Then, an old-fashioned bank safe in Jefferson City is cracked. The losses are high enough to bring the matter to Ben Price's attention.

Ben: *(To himself while reading newspaper stories about the burglaries)* That's Dandy Jim Valentine's autograph. He's resumed business. Look at that combination knob—jerked out as easy as pulling up a radish in wet weather. He's got the only clamps that can do it. Look how clean those tumblers were punched out! Jimmy never has to drill but one hole. Yes, I guess I want Mr. Valentine. He'll do his bit next time without any of this pardon foolishness.

First Narrator: One afternoon Jimmy Valentine steps down from a train in Elmore, a little town in Arkansas. He holds a suitcase in his hand.

Second Narrator: Jimmy, looking like an athletic senior just home from college, walks down the street. A young lady crosses the street towards him. Jimmy Valentine looks into her eyes and forgets who he is. She passes him at the corner and enters the Elmore Bank. Jimmy strikes up a conversation with a passerby and asks directions to a hotel. He also finds out that the young woman who caught his eye earlier is Annabel Adams, daughter of the owner of the Elmore Bank.

First Narrator:	Jimmy walks over to the Planters Hotel, signs in as Ralph D. Spencer, and asks for a room.
Second Narrator:	Then he leans over the desk and begins to talk to the hotel clerk.
Jimmy/Ralph:	I'm looking for a good location to set up a business. I've been thinking of going into the shoe business for some time now. How's the shoe business here? Are there any openings?
Hotel Clerk:	Yes, sir, Mr. Spencer. Elmore's a fine place to do business. I'm sure you can do quite well in the shoe business here. Elmore, you'll learn, is a pleasant town to live in. The people are very sociable and friendly.
Jimmy/Ralph:	Well, now, that's nice to hear. I guess I will stay over a few days and look the situation over. *(Reaches for his suitcase)*
Hotel Clerk:	May I have someone carry that to your room, Mr. Spencer?
Jimmy/Ralph:	No, thanks. I always carry the bag myself. It's a bit heavy.
First Narrator:	Mr. Ralph D. Spencer, also known as Jimmy Valentine, stays in Elmore and does very well for himself. He opens a successful shoe store. Socially he is also a success and makes many friends. He meets Miss Annabel Adams and becomes more and more captivated by her charms.

End of Act Three

Act Four

Second Narrator: Within a year, Mr. Ralph Spencer has won the respect of everyone in Elmore. His shoe store business has grown. He and Annabel are to be married in two weeks. One day Jimmy writes a letter, which he mails to one of his old friends in St. Louis.

Jimmy/Ralph: (*Reading*) Dear Old Pal: I want you to be at Sullivan's Place, in Little Rock, Wednesday night at nine o'clock. I want you to wind up some little matters for me. And, also, I want to make you a present of my kit of tools. Say, Billy, I quit the business a year ago. I've got a nice store. I'm making an honest living, and I'm going to marry the finest girl in the world. It's the only life, Billy—the honest one. I wouldn't touch a dollar of another person's money now for a million dollars. After I get married, I'm going to sell out and go West, where there won't be much danger of having old scores brought up against me. I tell you, Billy— she's an angel. She believes in me, and I wouldn't do another crooked thing for the whole world. Be sure to be at Sullivan's, for I must see you. I'll bring the tools with me.

First Narrator:	On the Monday night after Jimmy writes this letter, Ben Price arrives in Elmore.
Second Narrator:	He walks about town in his quiet way, until he finds out what he wants to know. From the drugstore across the street from Spencer's Shoe Store, he gets a good look at Ralph D. Spencer.
Ben:	*(To himself)* Going to marry the banker's daughter are you, Jimmy? Well, I don't know about that!
First Narrator:	The next morning, Jimmy has breakfast with the Adams family. He is going to Little Rock that day to order his wedding suit and to buy something nice for Annabel.
Second Narrator:	This will be the first time he has left town since coming to Elmore. It has been more than a year now since those last safecracking jobs, and he thinks he can safely travel out of town.
First Narrator:	After breakfast several members of the family go down to the bank together. In the group are Mr. Adams, Annabel, Jimmy, and Annabel's married sister, Jeanne, with her two little girls, ages five and nine.
Second Narrator:	Outside the bank stand Jimmy's horse and buggy and Dolph Gibson, who is going to drive him to the railroad station.

First Narrator: The family group goes inside the bank, where Jimmy sets his suitcase down. Annabel, whose heart is bubbling with happiness and lively youth, puts on Jimmy's hat and picks up the suitcase.

Annabel: Wouldn't I make a nice traveling saleslady? My, Ralph, how heavy your suitcase is. It feels like it is full of bricks.

Jimmy/Ralph: *(Quickly)* There are lots of nickel-plated shoehorns in there that I'm going to return. Thought I'd save express charges by taking them up myself. I'm getting awfully economical.

First Narrator: The Elmore Bank has a new safe and vault with a time lock. Mr. Adams is very proud of it and insists on an inspection by everyone. The two children, May and Agatha, are delighted by the shining metal and funny clock and knobs. While they are looking at the safe, Ben Price strolls in and leans on his elbow, looking around casually.

Second Narrator: Suddenly someone screams, and there is a commotion. Unseen by the elders, May, the nine-year-old, in a spirit of play, has shut Agatha in the vault. She turns the knob of the combination lock as she has seen Mr. Adams do.

Mr. Adams: *(Tugging at the vault handle)* The vault door can't be opened because the clock hasn't been wound and the combination lock hasn't been set!

First Narrator:	The screaming and commotion begin again.
Mr. Adams:	Everyone be quiet for a few minutes! Agatha, listen to me carefully and do as I say! Please remain very calm and do not panic!
Second Narrator:	During the following silence, they can just hear the faint sound of the child wildly shrieking in the dark vault in a panic of terror.
Jeanne:	*(Crying out)* My precious darling! She will die of fright! Open the door! Oh, break it down! Can't anything be done?
Mr. Adams:	There isn't anyone nearer than Little Rock who can open that door. That child—she can't stand it long in there! There isn't enough air! And besides, she'll go into convulsions from fright!
Jeanne:	*(Beating her hands against the vault door)* We must do something! Anything at all! Dynamite—dynamite the safe! We must not let Agatha die!
First Narrator:	Ralph D. Spencer, also known as Jimmy Valentine, barks an order.
Jimmy/Ralph:	Get away from the door, all of you!
Second Narrator:	He sets his suitcase on a table and opens it out flat. From that time on, he seems to be unconscious of the presence of anyone else. He lays out the shining instruments swiftly and orderly, whistling softly to himself as he always does when at work. In deep silence, the others watch him as if under a spell.

The Last Job

Mr. Adams:	*(Gruffly)* Mr. Spencer, what's going on here?
Annabel:	Hush, Father!
First Narrator:	In a minute, Jimmy's pet drill is biting smoothly into the steel door. In ten minutes, he throws open the door. Agatha, almost collapsed but safe, is gathered into her mother's arms.
Second Narrator:	His work done, Jimmy Valentine turns and walks toward the front door. At the door a big man stands somewhat in Jimmy's way.
Jimmy/Ralph:	Hello, Ben. Got around at last, have you? Well, let's go. I don't know that it makes much difference now.
Ben:	Guess you're mistaken, Mr. Spencer. Don't believe I recognize you. Your buggy's waiting for you, isn't it?
First Narrator:	With a tip of his hat, Ben Price turns and strolls into the street, leaving Jimmy Valentine wearing a strange smile on his face.

End of Play

The Last Job: What Do You Remember?

⭐ **Darken the letter by the correct answer.**

1. What kind of store does Jimmy Valentine open?
   - Ⓐ shoe store
   - Ⓑ safe store
   - Ⓒ buggy store
   - Ⓓ toy store

2. When does Jimmy Valentine become Ralph Spencer?
   - Ⓐ when he leaves prison
   - Ⓑ when he gets his tools at Sullivan's
   - Ⓒ when he moves to Elmore
   - Ⓓ when he saves Agatha

3. Jimmy strikes up a conversation with a man. What does *strikes up* mean?
   - Ⓐ hits
   - Ⓑ starts
   - Ⓒ bats
   - Ⓓ ends

4. The play is mostly about how
   - Ⓐ Jimmy is the best burglar ever.
   - Ⓑ a criminal can change and lead an honest life.
   - Ⓒ children should not be allowed in banks.
   - Ⓓ giving away burglar tools is not a good idea.

5. You can conclude that Jimmy thought
   - Ⓐ he would be sent back to prison.
   - Ⓑ he should not have saved Agatha.
   - Ⓒ the Adams' family knew who he really was.
   - Ⓓ he should not marry Annabel.

6. Why didn't Ben Price arrest Jimmy at the end?
   - Ⓐ He didn't know that Ralph Spencer was Jimmy Valentine.
   - Ⓑ He was tired of working that day.
   - Ⓒ He didn't like being a detective.
   - Ⓓ He thought Jimmy deserved a chance to change.

7. Why was Jimmy willing to open the bank vault even though he knew it might mean an end to his life as Ralph D. Spencer?

   _____

   _____

   _____

The Last Job: What's That Word?

⭐ Darken the circle by the vocabulary word that best completes each sentence.

1. Because Jimmy was sorry for the crimes he had done, he received a _____.
   - Ⓐ combination
   - Ⓑ pardon
   - Ⓒ convulsion
   - Ⓓ presence

2. The man bought a _____, well-made suit at the clothes store.
   - Ⓐ sociable
   - Ⓑ unconscious
   - Ⓒ captivated
   - Ⓓ tasteful

3. The woman _____ reading where she had stopped.
   - Ⓐ resumed
   - Ⓑ captivated
   - Ⓒ amalgamated
   - Ⓓ express

4. The cheap shoes were _____.
   - Ⓐ sociable
   - Ⓑ tumblers
   - Ⓒ economical
   - Ⓓ unconscious

5. The sick girl had such a high fever that it caused _____.
   - Ⓐ tumblers
   - Ⓑ pardon
   - Ⓒ casually
   - Ⓓ convulsions

6. He needs a _____ to open the safe lock.
   - Ⓐ combination
   - Ⓑ pardon
   - Ⓒ convulsion
   - Ⓓ presence

7. A person who is at ease acts _____.
   - Ⓐ captivated
   - Ⓑ casually
   - Ⓒ unconscious
   - Ⓓ economical

8. An available job at a business is called an _____.
   - Ⓐ express
   - Ⓑ economical
   - Ⓒ amalgamated
   - Ⓓ opening

9. Someone who gets along well with other people is _____.
   - Ⓐ tasteful
   - Ⓑ sociable
   - Ⓒ resumed
   - Ⓓ economical

10. Someone who is attracted to another's charms is _____.
   - Ⓐ presence
   - Ⓑ unconscious
   - Ⓒ captivated
   - Ⓓ express

The Last Job: What Do You Think?

The prison system in this country costs taxpayers millions of dollars each year. It costs a lot of money to lock up a criminal. At the same time, people who fear being victims of crime want to feel safe.

Sometimes, criminals receive pardons. That means they are excused or forgiven for the crimes they have committed. Are pardons a good idea? Should people who commit crimes against others receive pardons?

 Complete the chart. Write at least three reasons for and three reasons against pardoning criminals.

Reasons for Pardons	Reasons Against Pardons

 ## *The Last Job:* Write Away!

Decide whether you are for or against pardons. Then use your reasons in the chart to write a persuasive essay. Convince the reader that your opinion is correct.

A Star To Guide You

Meet the Players

Character	Reading Level
Narrator	5.3
Kevin Jackson, *a ninth-grade student*	4.9
Bob Jackson, *his father*	4.3
Janet Jackson, *his mother*	2.5
Martha Jackson, *his sister*	2.0
Doug Jackson, *his younger brother*	2.0
Mr. Walker, *a shop teacher*	5.0
Jane Lee, *a student in Mr. Walker's shop class*	2.5
Richie Cohen, *a student in Mr. Walker's shop class*	4.2

Play Summary

Kevin Jackson is upset by his parents' recent separation and angrily destroys a Christmas display. He is caught in the act by the owner of the display, Mr. Walker, a vocational arts teacher at Kevin's school. Kevin is ashamed of what he has done and readily agrees to help rebuild the display. While working on the project, Kevin comes to realize he is not the only person who has had sadness enter his life. Mr. Walker, who has been divorced, teaches Kevin he can find happiness in life once he learns how to "turn something hurting into something positive."

Vocabulary

nativity, pp. 50, 53
clam up, p. 52
glares, p. 52
elbow grease, p. 55
drill presses, p. 56

figured, p. 58
scroll saw, p. 58
project, pp. 58, 60
nova, p. 60
Jewish, p. 61

split up, p. 62
positive, pp. 62, 63
brackets, p. 64
awesome, p. 65
thumbs up, p. 65

Tapping Prior Knowledge

Before reading the play, discuss these questions with students.

1. Have you ever done something out of anger that you later regretted? Explain your answer.

2. What do you think should happen to a person who destroys someone else's property?

3. Have you ever had someone promise to do something with you and then back out of the promise? How did you feel? What did you say or do?

A Star To Guide You

Thinking It Over

The following questions may be used for oral discussion or as written exercises.

1. What reasons did Kevin's mother give for getting a divorce?

2. When Mr. Walker asked Kevin why he had destroyed the Christmas display, Kevin told Mr. Walker that he just felt like doing it. Was Kevin being completely truthful, or did he have another reason? Explain your answer.

3. What does Kevin learn from Jane Lee and Richie Cohen?

4. What did Mr. Walker make for Kevin? Why do you think Mr. Walker made it?

Presenting the Play

Radio Play: Use these sound effects to present *A Star To Guide You* as a radio play.

- taped music to indicate act breaks—pp. 49, 51, 52, 55, 57, 59, 60, 63
- knock on door—Act One, p. 49
- car door opening and closing—Act Two, pp. 50, 51
- car engine running—Act Two, pp. 50, 51; Act Eight, p. 61; Act Nine, p. 65
- school bell—Act Five, pp. 55, 57
- car/truck horns—Act Nine, p. 64

Classroom Play: To stage the play in a classroom, use the sound effects listed for the radio play and the props listed below.

- chairs for car seats—Act Two, pp. 50–52
- cardboard silhouettes for Christmas display—Act Two, pp. 50, 51; Act Four, pp. 53–55; Act Eight, pp. 60, 61; Act Nine, pp. 63–64
- table and chairs for kitchen—Act Three, p. 52; Act Eight, pp. 62–63
- table, blanket, and pillow for bed—Act Four, p. 53
- tools and tables for shop class—Act Five, pp. 55–57; Act Six, pp. 58–59; Act Seven, p. 60; Act Eight, p. 61
- sheets of plywood (or cardboard)—Act Five, pp. 56–57; Act Six, pp. 58–59, Act Seven, p. 60
- grapes—Act Five, p. 57
- birdhouse/tie rack—Act Six, p. 58
- pencil—Act Six, p. 59
- Christmas star cutout—Act Seven, p. 60; Act Eight, p. 61; Act Nine, p. 65
- trays of cookies—Act Eight, pp. 62–63
- photographs—Act Nine, pp. 64–65

Extending the Play

Use these activities to enrich the students' reading of *A Star To Guide You.*

1. Use any or all of the blackline masters on pages 164–168.

2. Have students draw a picture of Mr. Walker's Christmas display.

3. Have students make a list of more appropriate ways Kevin could have used to deal with his anger.

READERS' THEATER II

Presents

A STAR TO GUIDE YOU

by
Peggy Nicholson

Cast

(in order of appearance)

Narrator

Martha Jackson, *Kevin Jackson's younger sister*

Doug Jackson, *Kevin's younger brother*

Kevin Jackson, *a ninth-grade student*

Bob Jackson, *Kevin's father*

Janet Jackson, *Kevin's mother*

Mr. Walker, *a shop teacher*

Jane Lee
Richie Cohen } *students in Mr. Walker's shop class*

Act One

Narrator: Kevin, Doug, and Martha Jackson are waiting for their father in the living room. When he knocks on the front door, Martha runs to answer it.

Martha: *(Opening the door)* He's here! He's here! Daddy's here!

Doug: Gee, Dad, you don't have to knock.

Kevin: *(To himself)* But he does have to knock. That's the whole problem.

Narrator: Bob Jackson, their father, had moved out of the house just after Thanksgiving. And now there are just two weeks until Christmas, and their parents still have not made up.

Bob: Well, are you ready to see the lights?

Narrator: It has been a Jackson family tradition to drive around town each year to look at Christmas decorations. But this year the idea makes Kevin sick.

Kevin: Mom! Mom! Are you sure you don't want to come?

Janet: *(Entering the room)* No, thanks. *(To Bob Jackson)* It's a school night. Please don't keep them out late.

End of Act One

Act Two

Narrator: In the car Martha sits up front where her mother should have been. Kevin and Doug sit in the back, not looking at each other. Bob Jackson drives slowly and points out all the decorations. His voice is loud and cheerful.

Bob: Gee, look at that house! They must have half a mile of lights strung up. That's pretty neat, right, Kevin?

Kevin: *(Grumpily)* Yes, I guess so.

Narrator: But Kevin is wondering why his mother wears an old sweatshirt and jeans when she knows his dad is coming by. He is also wondering why she doesn't just try a little to make up with his dad.

Bob: Martha, which do you like? The house with blue lights or that pink, flashing number?

Martha: I don't care. Daddy, what about Christmas? You're going to open presents with us, right?

Bob: Well, honey, I hadn't really thought about it. Say, will you look at that! Old Mr. Walker's done it again. That's the best house in town. Don't you agree, Doug?

Doug: You say that every year, Dad. But what about Christmas? It won't be the same if you're not there.

Narrator: The house they are driving past is lit with what seems like a million red and green lights. On the front lawn are a whole choir of wooden angels, a troop of tin soldiers, and a life-size nativity scene. Kevin has always liked the wooden cutouts of the donkey and the ox and the lamb. The Wise Men have crowns of tiny, blinking lights.

Bob: Look at Santa's reindeer on the roof, Martha. And Santa himself is climbing into the chimney. He's a work of art. Did I tell you Mr. Walker was my shop teacher my last year in school, Kev? He's quite a guy.

Kevin: You told me. Seems pretty silly to me, making such a fuss about Christmas. It's nothing but plywood. Who cares?

Martha: I do! Please, Daddy, say you'll come open presents with us.

Bob: Martha, what can I—I'll try. But . . .

Doug: All right! I knew you would!

Martha: Oh, Daddy, thank you! I love you!

Narrator: Bob Jackson doesn't say much on the drive home. When he parks in the driveway, he stays in the car. Martha and Doug run into the house to tell their mother the good news.

Bob: Kev, I don't think it's a good idea for me to come to the house for Christmas. But I want you kids to stay with me the weekend after. We'll celebrate New Year's Eve together. We'll do something special, like go out to supper and a movie. Does that sound okay?

Kevin: But . . . but . . .

Bob: It's the best thing, believe me, Kev. Now, will you tell Martha and Doug? Tell them we'll really have a super time. I promise.

End of Act Two

Act Three

Narrator: When Kevin goes into the house, he finds Martha in the kitchen with their mother.

Martha: I'm glad Daddy's coming here for Christmas. Aren't you, Mom? Everything's going to be okay, isn't it?

Kevin: Dad's not coming, Martha. So you can just clam up about it. He changed his mind.

Martha: But he can't! He promised! He promised!

Narrator: Martha runs out of the room in tears, and Janet Jackson glares at Kevin. Then she goes after Martha.

Kevin: *(To himself)* Yes, well, he broke his promise. He broke all the promises. Merry Christmas!

Narrator: Kevin goes to his room. In a few minutes, his mother looks in on him.

Janet: Kevin, I know why you're angry, but . . .

Kevin: Why can't you and Dad make up? It's Christmas! Doesn't that mean anything to you?

Janet: Kev, we have made up, but that doesn't mean we're getting back together. If you could just understand. We married so young—just out of high school. We didn't really know who we were, what we wanted, or what love really is.

Kevin: I don't want to hear this. Please go away.

End of Act Three

Act Four

Narrator: After his mother is gone, Kevin lies on his bed for a long time, but he can't sleep. Finally, he climbs out the window and goes for a walk. He walks a long time. The streets are dark and quiet. When he finally looks up, he is standing in front of Mr. Walker's house with its wonderful decorations blinking at him.

Kevin: What are you smiling at, you stupid donkey?

Narrator: The donkey in the nativity scene does seem to be grinning at Kevin. It seems as if it knows Christmas is only a bad joke. So Kevin kicks the donkey in the stomach, and it falls over. He turns and finds the ox giving him a sad look. So he knocks it over, too. And the Wise Men look shocked. He punches one in the nose, and it hurts him so much Kevin's eyes begin to water.

Kevin: Stupid, rotten Christmas! Who cares?

Narrator: The next thing he knows, he is scrambling up a tree and climbing onto the roof of Mr. Walker's house. He grabs a reindeer, snaps off its antlers, and hurls it to the ground. Then he runs at Santa.

Kevin: It's your fault!

Narrator: He breaks off Santa's head and is trying to stuff it down the chimney when someone calls to him.

Mr. Walker: You! Kid! What do you think you're doing? Get down here—now!

Narrator: Kevin has never been so scared. He looks at the head of Santa he is holding, and he can hardly believe what he's done. His hand is bleeding, but he doesn't know how or when he cut it. He climbs down the tree. Mr. Walker sure doesn't look happy.

Mr. Walker: Why did you wreck my decorations, kid?

Kevin: I don't know. I don't have a reason.

Mr. Walker: No reason! You go nuts for no reason? *(Pauses)* Say, you're one of Bob Jackson's kids, aren't you?

Kevin: You . . . know me?

Mr. Walker: I've seen you around the school cafeteria. You're a ninth-grader, right?

Kevin: Yes, sir.

Mr. Walker: *(Holding Santa's head)* What's your dad going to say about this? Does he know the reason you're beating up on Christmas?

Kevin: No, sir! There isn't any reason. I just felt like doing it. But please don't bother my father. He's got a lot of stuff on his mind right now. *(Almost in tears)* Please?

Mr. Walker: He does? Then I guess this is just between you and me. *(Pauses)* How many days until Christmas vacation? Nine? Have you got a study hall, Mr. No Reason?

Kevin: Yes, sir. I have study hall just before lunch.

Mr. Walker: Good. I'll see you in shop tomorrow, kid. Bring a bucket of elbow grease. And don't be late!

Act Five

Narrator: The next day, when the bell for his study hall rings, Kevin finds himself trudging down the hall to the shop classroom. He pushes open the door and stands just inside, scared to move any farther. But no one even looks up. It is the busiest, noisiest classroom Kevin has ever been in. Students are hammering, sawing, drilling, or slipping into safety goggles and dust masks. A girl comes out of a supply closet and bumps into Kevin.

Kevin: Sorry. Hey, have you seen Mr. Walker?

Jane: Sure, he's over here. Come on.

Narrator: The girl leads Kevin between shop tables, around table saws, and past a row of drill presses. She stops by a table where Mr. Walker and a student are setting one of the broken reindeer on top of a sheet of plywood.

Jane: Have you heard about what some guys did to Mr. Walker's Christmas display?

Kevin: *(Nervously)* Yes, I heard.

Mr. Walker: There you are. Jane and Richie, this is a neighbor of mine. He volunteered to help fix the decorations. Care to show him what to do, Richie?

Richie: Sure thing, Mr. Walker.

Narrator: Mr. Walker hurries away to help another student adjust a table-saw blade.

Richie: You got a name?

Kevin: Yes, it's Kevin. Kevin Jackson.

Richie: Okay, Kevin, so let's get a move on. We'll use the old reindeer as a guide to make the new ones. We'll have to draw the antlers freehand, though. They were broken off.

Narrator: As they work, Kevin notices Mr. Walker gives Richie a satisfied nod. Then Mr. Walker glances at Kevin, and his smile vanishes. Mr. Walker turns to walk away when the bell rings.

Richie: It's time for lunch! You coming, Kevin?

Narrator: Kevin is hungry, but he looks up and sees Mr. Walker watching him again.

Kevin: No, thanks, Richie. Mr. Walker, is it okay if I stay through lunch? I've got two more reindeer to trace.

Narrator: Mr. Walker doesn't smile, but his face doesn't look quite so stern.

Mr. Walker: Sure, kid. I'll be in my office. Call if you need any help.

Narrator: In a little while, Mr. Walker wanders out of his office. He stops beside Kevin and holds out a bag of grapes.

Mr. Walker: I thought I heard a stomach growling out here.

Narrator: Kevin takes a grape—just one.

Kevin: Thanks, Mr. Walker. And thanks for not telling everyone I'm the one who did all this.

Narrator: Mr. Walker doesn't answer. He puts some more grapes on the table by Kevin and strolls back into his office.

End of Act Five

Act Six

Narrator: The next day Kevin finds it easier to walk into shop class. Jane looks up from her project and smiles.

Jane: What do you think of my birdhouse, Kevin?

Kevin: That's not a birdhouse. It's an apartment—a castle!

Jane: Well, my stepfather likes birds. I figured this would attract a whole flock.

Kevin: You even shingled the roof. It's neat!

Jane: Come see the tie rack I made for my other dad— my real dad.

Narrator: She shows him the tie rack, gleaming with varnish. It is as nice as her birdhouse. Kevin doesn't know which gift would please him more if he were one of Jane's fathers.

Richie: Hey, Kev, let's go! Mr. Walker says to show you how to use a scroll saw.

Narrator: By the end of the period, Kevin has roughed out the shape of one reindeer's antlers. Blowing on a blistered thumb, he watches the other kids hurry off to lunch.

Kevin: I'll never finish these reindeer by the start of Christmas vacation. And I still have the Santa, and then there are the Wise Men!

Mr. Walker: Now that you know the hard way, care to learn a shortcut?

Narrator: Mr. Walker spends the rest of his lunch break teaching Kevin how to use a power jigsaw. At first, it is a bit scary; then it is easy and fun. With half of the reindeer cut out, Kevin stops while he and Mr. Walker turn the plywood sheet and clamp it down again.

Kevin: Mr. Walker, I want to say I'm sorry. You must have worked hours and hours—years even—making all these decorations. I'm going to replace every one, even if it takes me until Easter.

Mr. Walker: Glad to hear that, kid. But I'd still like to know why you did it. I taught your father. He was always a good kid—responsible. So what got into you?

Kevin: *(Angrily)* Yes, Dad's responsible all right. So responsible he walked out on his family.

Mr. Walker: Is that so?

Narrator: He pats Kevin's shoulder as if he is thinking about something else. When Kevin goes back to sawing, Mr. Walker strolls over to a new sheet of plywood. He takes a pencil from behind his ear and begins sketching on the wood.

End of Act Six

Act Seven

Narrator: The next day Jane goes over to Kevin's table.

Jane: I'm done with my birdhouse, Kevin. Need some help?

Narrator: With Jane and Kevin sawing and Richie painting the figures as they are finished, the work goes quickly. Meanwhile, Mr. Walker works on his own project nearby. He is cutting a huge, lacy shape.

Richie: What's that, Mr. Walker? Is it a giant snowflake?

Mr. Walker: Why, this is a star, Richie. Can't you tell?

Jane: *(Laughing)* That's no star, Mr. Walker. That's a nova!

Act Eight

Narrator: Whatever it is, Mr. Walker keeps working on it for the next few days. Meanwhile, Kevin, Richie, and Jane turn out a whole herd of glossy, brown reindeer.

Kevin: Well, today's the last day. You think Mr. Walker will let me stay after school? I've still got Santa to do, and the Wise Men need painting.

Richie: I bet he will. He's still working on his crazy star. And I can stay and help, too.

Kevin: That would be great, Richie. But how come I never see you working on any Christmas gifts?

Richie: Well, I'm Jewish. We don't celebrate Christmas in our house. But I did make Dad a pipe rack for his birthday next week. I don't have to worry about gifts for a mother. Mine died when I was three. *(Pauses)* So anyway, let's get a move on. You get the saws, and I'll set up Santa.

Narrator: Kevin keeps thinking the rest of the day about what Richie said. Kevin knows he is learning something. Behind every person's smile, there's also a sad story to tell.

Kevin: *(To himself)* I wonder if there is a sad story behind Mr. Walker's smile.

Narrator: Kevin gets a chance to find out when they finish the last figure. Being careful not to damage the paint, they load the reindeer, Santa, and Mr. Walker's monstrous star onto his truck. Richie, who lives nearby, walks off towards home with a smile and a wave.

Richie: See you tomorrow!

Narrator: Mr. Walker gives Jane and Kevin a ride home. After he lets Jane off, he and Kevin ride in silence. Then Kevin looks back at the big star.

Kevin: How come you do this Christmas show, Mr. Walker? It's got to be a lot of trouble setting it up every year.

Mr. Walker: Funny, I never thought of it that way, but I guess it is. Let's see. I started about ten years ago. My wife and I split up that fall, and I had a lot of time on my hands. I didn't want to sit around feeling blue, so I looked for something to cheer myself up. I hope it brings cheer to others, too.

Kevin: It always makes my family smile when we drive by at Christmas.

Mr. Walker: You want to try to turn something hurting into something positive, Kevin. Do that, and things will work out. One day when you're not even expecting it, happiness will come sneaking up behind you and tap you on the shoulder.

Narrator: After Mr. Walker drops Kevin off, Kevin goes into his house. A wonderful smell greets him as he walks through the door.

Kevin: I smell cookies!

Narrator: In the kitchen, his mother stands at the counter, rolling out dough. She has smudges of flour on her face. There are two trays of cookies in the oven, and two more waiting to be baked.

Kevin: *(To himself)* She's turning a hurt into something positive. Well, if she can do it, maybe I can, too. *(To his mother)* Want some help, Mom?

Janet: Sure! I'll bake, and you can decorate.

Narrator: While Kevin makes zigzags and circles with red and green icing, he remembers a joke Richie told him in school. He tells it to his mother, and she laughs. He hasn't heard that sound for weeks. Then Martha and Doug come in.

Martha: Cookies! Can I make some?

Doug: I want to do something, too! Let me help with the icing, Kev.

Narrator: So they all sit around the kitchen table, laughing and making Christmas cookies until long after their regular bedtime. It is the best time Kevin remembers in months.

End of Act Eight

Act Nine

Narrator: The next day is Saturday, the first day of Christmas vacation. When Kevin walks over to Mr. Walker's house, Jane and Richie are waiting for him.

Richie: Come on, Kevin! Get a move on! We're doing the manger scene first. Here, help me set up this cow.

Jane: That's an ox, Richie. Now, who wants some of Mr. Walker's hot apple cider?

Richie: Hey, Mr. Walker, where does the donkey go?

Narrator: As they work, lots of cars go by. Drivers honk or wave. People are happy to see the Christmas show going up again—Kevin most of all. They place half the reindeer on the roof. Then Kevin and Mr. Walker go inside the house for some more screws and mounting brackets.

Mr. Walker: Oh, Kevin, take a look at this. See anyone you know?

Narrator: A row of photographs hangs along one wall. Each is a picture of a group of smiling kids. They are posed in Mr. Walker's classroom. He taps one photo.

Kevin: No, I don't think . . . *(Squinting)* Is that my dad?

Mr. Walker: It sure is. He was a senior there. He's filled out some since then, hasn't he?

Kevin: *(Surprised)* He doesn't look any older than I do!

Narrator:	In the picture, Bob Jackson is just a kid, with a silly haircut and a goofy grin. Then Kevin remembers that his dad married his mom just after they graduated.
Kevin:	*(To himself)* Maybe Mom was right. They were too young to get married.
Narrator:	The picture makes Kevin happy and also sad. It makes him want to hug his dad—or the teenager in the photo. When he goes back outside, Jane and Richie are still up on the roof.
Richie:	Think we're all done up here, except maybe for your super star. Where does it go, Mr. Walker?
Mr. Walker:	It goes on Kevin's roof. I made it for him.
Narrator:	Kevin doesn't know what to say. But the twinkle in Mr. Walker's eye says he reads Kevin's smile loud and clear.
Jane:	Well, let's go, then!
Narrator:	They drive to Kevin's house and put the star on the roof. Then they all stand back to admire it.
Kevin:	*(Softly)* It's—it's awesome!
Narrator:	Kevin feels a light tap on his shoulder. As he turns to look, he almost thinks it could be happiness sneaking up on him. But it is just Mr. Walker, giving a thumbs up sign and grinning.
Mr. Walker:	Merry Christmas, kid!

End of Play

A Star To Guide You: What Do You Remember?

⭐ **Darken the letter by the correct answer.**

1. What does Mr. Walker teach?
   - Ⓐ English
   - Ⓑ history
   - Ⓒ shop
   - Ⓓ P.E.

2. When did Kevin destroy Mr. Walker's decorations?
   - Ⓐ after he met Jane and Richie
   - Ⓑ after his father said he wouldn't come for Christmas
   - Ⓒ after he helped his mother bake cookies
   - Ⓓ after Mr. Walker made a star

3. Kevin used a scroll saw to make reindeer antlers. What is a scroll saw?
   - Ⓐ an exercise machine
   - Ⓑ a cookie cutter
   - Ⓒ a type of wood
   - Ⓓ a tool used to cut wood into special designs

4. The play is mostly about
   - Ⓐ turning something hurting into something positive.
   - Ⓑ making Christmas decorations.
   - Ⓒ making new friends.
   - Ⓓ doing well in school.

5. You can conclude that Kevin
   - Ⓐ will want to get married at a young age.
   - Ⓑ will want to become a house decorator.
   - Ⓒ will stay angry with his parents.
   - Ⓓ will try to enjoy Christmas, no matter what happens.

6. The next time Kevin is angry and upset, he will probably
   - Ⓐ destroy something else.
   - Ⓑ make another star.
   - Ⓒ try to make the best of it.
   - Ⓓ run away from home.

7. Why did Jane make a birdhouse and a tie rack?

   _____

   _____

   _____

A *Star To Guide You*: What's That Word?

★ **Read the sentences from the story. Think about the meanings of the words in bold type.**

★ On the front lawn are a whole choir of wooden angels, a troop of tin soldiers, and a life-size **nativity** scene. Kevin has always liked the wooden cutouts of the donkey and the ox and the lamb. The Wise Men have crowns of tiny, blinking lights.

★ While working on the **project,** Kevin comes to realize he is not the only person who has had sadness enter his life.

★ My wife and I **split up** that fall, and I had a lot of time on my hands.

★ Well, my stepfather likes birds. I **figured** this would attract a whole flock.

★ You want to try to turn something hurting into something **positive,** Kevin.

★ Dad's not coming, Martha. So you can just **clam up** about it. He changed his mind.

★ Then Kevin and Mr. Walker go inside the house for some more screws and mounting **brackets.**

★ Martha runs out of the room in tears, and Janet Jackson **glares** at Kevin.

★ I'll see you in shop tomorrow, kid. Bring a bucket of **elbow grease**. And don't be late!

★ Kevin feels a light tap on his shoulder. As he turns to look, he almost thinks it could be happiness sneaking up on him. But it is just Mr. Walker, giving a **thumbs up** sign and grinning.

★ **Use clues in the sentences to figure out the meaning of each word. Write each word on the line next to its meaning.**

_____ **1.** metal supports

_____ **2.** a sign of hope and encouragement

_____ **3.** hard physical work

_____ **4.** having to do with the birth of Jesus Christ

_____ **5.** to divorce or break up

_____ **6.** a special undertaking

_____ **7.** to scowl or stare with anger

_____ **8.** to become silent or stop talking

_____ **9.** better; helpful; useful

_____ **10.** concluded or thought

A Star To Guide You: What Do You Think?

⭐ Make a decoration for a different holiday or season. Use the grid below to draw a pattern. Then, make a larger image on poster board. Increase the size of the grid squares on the poster board.

<table>
<tr><td></td><td></td><td></td><td></td></tr>
<tr><td></td><td></td><td></td><td></td></tr>
<tr><td></td><td></td><td></td><td></td></tr>
<tr><td></td><td></td><td></td><td></td></tr>
</table>

A Star To Guide You: Write Away!

Write another act to the play. Tell how Kevin's family spends the rest of the holiday season.

JUAN'S STORY

Meet the Players

Character	Reading Level
Narrator	5.0
Juan Villa, *a teenage boy*	5.0
Manuela Villa, *his mother*	2.1
Jorge Villa, *his father*	2.1
José Gabón, *Juan's friend*	2.0
Fred Willis, *Juan's friend*	2.0
Lisa Brown, *Juan's friend*	2.2
Judd Burns, *community center director*	2.3
Annie, *a swim coach*	4.6
Announcer	2.0

Play Summary

Juan Villa feels like an outcast because of his disability. He walks with a pronounced limp, which is the result of a bicycle accident. A classmate convinces Juan to join a beginner's swim class. The swim coach, Annie, and Juan are at odds from day one. Nonetheless, Juan finds that he has a talent for swimming and begins to enjoy his classes. When Juan enters a swim meet, Annie accuses him of settling for second best instead of trying to win. Juan is furious. He lashes back at Annie with a self-pitying outburst, totally unaware that Annie, too, has a disability. When the director of the community center points out that Annie is deaf, Juan realizes he has been unfair to her and apologizes. Annie and Juan at last understand each other.

Vocabulary

tough, p. 74
altogether, p. 74
bitterly, p. 75
abruptly, p. 75
treat, p. 75

center, p. 77
scornfully, p. 79
sharp, p. 79
outstretched, p. 83
deafening, p. 85

freestyle, p. 85
occurs, p. 86
momentarily, p. 87
snubbed, p. 88
disability, p. 89

Tapping Prior Knowledge

Before reading the play, discuss these questions with students.

1. Do you like competition? Why or why not?

2. Have you ever formed an opinion about someone before you got to know him or her? Did your opinion turn out to be correct?

3. Have you ever felt left out? Describe the situation. What did you say and do?

Teacher Notes

JUAN'S STORY

Thinking It Over

The following questions may be used for oral discussion or as written exercises.

1. Why did Juan feel sorry for himself?

2. Why did Juan work hard even though he disliked Annie?

3. Why was Juan satisfied when he finished second in the swim race? Should he have been satisfied? Explain your answer.

4. What do you think Annie meant when she said that everybody has a disability, one way or another?

Presenting the Play

Radio Play: Use these sound effects to present *Juan's Story* as a radio play.

- taped music to indicate act breaks— pp. 74, 75, 77, 80, 81, 83, 84
- door opening and closing—Act Two, p. 74
- door slamming—Act Two, p. 75
- water splashing—Act Four, pp. 78, 79

- whistle blowing—Act Four, p. 80; Act Five, p. 81
- noisy crowd—Act Nine, p. 85
- sound of gun firing—Act Nine, pp. 86, 87
- crowd cheering—Act Nine, p. 87

Classroom Play: To stage the play in the classroom, use the sound effects listed for the radio play and the props listed below.

- softball, bats, gloves— Act One, p. 73
- table, chairs, cups, saucers— Act Two, p. 74
- swimsuit—Act Four, p. 78
- whistle—Act Four, p. 80; Act Five, p. 81

- chairs arranged as rows on a school bus—Act Eight, p. 84
- chairs arranged as bleachers in a gymnasium—Act Nine, pp. 85–88
- starting gun—Act Nine, pp. 86, 87

Extending the Play

Use these activities to enrich the students' experience with readers' theater.

1. Use any or all of the blackline masters on pages 164–168.

2. Tell students to imagine they are Juan. Have them write a thank-you note to Judd Burns for allowing Juan to join the swim team.

3. Tell students to imagine they are Annie. Have them write a diary entry about the day of the swim meet.

4. Have students make a medal or trophy to present to their favorite character.

READERS' THEATER II

Presents

JUAN'S STORY

by
Jack Warner

Cast

(in order of appearance)

Narrator

José Gabón, *Juan's friend*

Fred Willis, *Juan's friend*

Lisa Brown, *Juan's friend*

Juan Villa, *a teenage boy*

Manuela Villa, *Juan's mother*

Jorge Villa, *Juan's father*

Judd Burns, *community center director*

Annie, *a swim coach*

Announcer

Act One

Narrator: The children in King Park are picking players for a softball game. José Gabón, captain of one team, and Fred Willis, captain of the other, are doing the choosing.

José: I'll take Pete.

Fred: Give me Cappy.

José: Lisa's mine.

Fred: I get Kim.

José: Let's see, now. That's all the players, right?

Fred: We have eight on each side. Each team will have only two outfielders, but that's the best we can do.

Narrator: Juan Villa stands to one side, watching. Nobody has picked him. But then he hadn't expected to be chosen. He guesses no one wants a player with a bad leg on a softball team.

Lisa: *(Calling)* Hey, Juan!

Juan: Yes?

Lisa: Do you want to umpire?

Juan: No, I don't know anything about umpiring.

Narrator: Lisa and the others watch as Juan turns away and walks off the field.

Fred: Wouldn't he do it?

José: No, and that's too bad. You'd think he'd want to do something. At least talk and hang around and watch the game.

Lisa: Take it easy, guys. It's not easy being Juan these days.

Act Two

Narrator: Juan slowly makes his way home. He enters the apartment through the back door, hoping to avoid his parents. But they are both sitting in the kitchen.

Juan: Hi. José and Fred and the others started playing a softball game and . . .

Manuela: Oh, Juan, my poor Juan!

Juan: Cut it out, will you please? It's bad enough without . . .

Jorge: Look, Juan, I know things seem tough right now. But you have to look at the good side. You were lucky. You could have been killed when that car knocked you off your bike. Or you might have lost your leg altogether. Don't forget that, Juan. You are lucky.

Juan: (*Bitterly*) Lucky! Is two years of being in and out of the hospital and having five operations lucky? I'll probably never play ball or ride a bike again. And school . . .

Jorge: Enough, Juan! You have a long life ahead of you. Don't ruin it with bitterness. There are many things you can do. But you must do them yourself. You must want to do them.

Narrator: Juan turns abruptly and starts for his room. He goes into his room and slams the door behind him.

Jorge: (*Angrily*) Juan!

Manuela: Let him go, Jorge. He's sad.

Jorge: Manuela, we mustn't treat Juan like a baby. That's bad for him. You and I mustn't treat him differently. We must think of Juan as he was.

Manuela: Yes, Jorge, we've both been wrong. We, too, must be strong.

Jorge: Why did he talk about school, Manuela? Isn't he doing well?

Manuela: For two years, Jorge, Juan has had a teacher come to the house to help him keep up with his schoolwork. Now the principal wants Juan back in school.

Jorge: But that's good news.

Manuela: It is, Jorge. I know it is. But I don't know how he will feel about that. He's so shy. I hope it all works out.

End of Act Two

Act Three

Narrator: The following Monday afternoon, Juan is walking home from school alone. It has been a hard day for him. It seems as if everyone is treating him, well, differently somehow. He thinks he can see it in their eyes. "Poor Juan," they seem to be saying. He is angry and hurt. That is when Lisa Brown catches up to him.

Lisa: You look like a guy who just lost his only friend. Are you feeling okay, Juan?

Juan: Yes, I guess so, Lisa. It's just that . . .

Lisa: You're mad. Because of the accident and all.

Juan: How did you know?

Lisa: *(Laughing)* How did I know? Because it shows all over you, that's how I know. *(Pauses)* Hey, Juan, do you ever go swimming?

Juan: No.

Lisa: Care to give it a try?

Juan: Where?

Lisa: At the community center. It's cool, Juan. Come on, I'll take you there.

Juan: I know the place. You mean there's a swimming pool in there?

Lisa: Yes, there is. Maybe you didn't know, but the community center is the home of just about the best swim club in southern California.

Act Four

Narrator: Lisa leads Juan to the community center, where she introduces him to the director.

Judd: Hi, I'm Judd Burns. I'm the director of the center. What did you say your name is?

Juan: *(Shyly)* Juan, Mr. Burns. Juan Villa.

Lisa: He wants to join a swim class, Mr. Burns.

Juan: Well, I don't have a swimsuit. I . . . I can't even swim. I don't know how.

Judd: Don't worry, Juan. We always have extra swimsuits around. We even have a beginner's class, too. I'm sure we can squeeze one more into the pool. Come with me, and we'll get you set up right now.

Lisa: I'll talk to you later, Juan. *(Laughing)* Smile, buddy. You'll love swimming!

Narrator: In minutes Juan has changed into the swimsuit Judd Burns has given him. Juan stuffs his clothes into a locker and walks through the door to the pool.

Judd: *(Smiling)* Hey, that swimsuit fits perfectly. In fact, it looks like it was made just for you. Ready to start?

Juan: I don't have any money for lessons.

Judd: Did I say anything about paying?

Juan: I don't need your charity.

Judd: Whoa there, Juan. What charity? Anyone can join the community pool free. *(Pauses)* Well, are you staying?

Juan: I . . . I guess so.

Narrator: At the other end of the pool, a slim girl a few years older than Juan is shouting at a group of swimmers in the water. They are holding on to the edge of the pool and kicking their feet.

Annie: Kick harder! You're never going to learn to swim until you learn how to kick. You'll sink to the bottom like rocks.

Narrator: Judd Burns leads Juan over to Annie. He walks up behind her and taps her on the shoulder. She turns around and faces the director.

Judd: I've got another live one for you, Annie. This is Juan Villa. Think you can teach him how to swim?

Annie: Sure, if he works at it.

Juan: *(To Judd Burns)* Is she the teacher?

Judd: Yes, and she's one of the best. She's the county champ in the 50-meter backstroke. We call her Too-Fast Annie.

Narrator: After Judd Burns leaves, Annie looks at Juan scornfully, with her hands on her hips.

Annie: What's wrong with you? You don't think you can learn from a girl?

Juan: I don't know. I have a bad leg.

Annie: So what? That's no excuse. Well, are you going into the water or not? Make up your mind fast because I haven't got all day.

Narrator: Angered by Annie's sharp words, Juan slips into the water. It is cold at first, and he holds his breath. Then he begins to like it as he gets used to it.

Annie: *(Yelling)* Okay, everybody, get back to your kicking. You're not at a picnic, you know. That goes for you, too, Wayne.

Narrator: It takes Juan a few seconds to realize that Annie is talking to him.

Juan: *(Shouting)* Juan! My name is Juan, not Wayne!

Narrator: Annie doesn't seem to pay any attention to him. But Juan soon forgets about that. He finds he is enjoying himself. He can kick easily in the water. He is as good as anyone else and maybe better than some.

Annie: *(Blowing her whistle)* That's enough for today. You can stay in the water for ten more minutes. But don't leave the shallow end. I don't want to have to pull some turkey out.

Narrator: They all laugh at that. Juan is enjoying himself so much he is disappointed when the whistle blows again. But, like the others, he climbs out of the pool. Annie faces him.

Annie: Lessons are Mondays, Wednesdays, and Fridays at four o'clock sharp. Will you be here, Wayne?

Juan: I guess I will if I don't have something more important to do. *(Walking away from Annie)* But my name is Juan, not Wayne!

End of Act Four

Act Five

Narrator: Wednesday arrives, and Juan is at the pool. By the end of the second week, he is far ahead of everyone else in his class. He can float and do a few strokes. He even swims across the pool on his own. Annie says nothing, but Judd Burns looks happy.

Judd: You're doing great, Juan! You sure like to swim, don't you?

Juan: *(Holding back his excitement)* Oh, it's okay, I guess.

Judd: Starting today we'll have an extra hour of swimming just for the swimmers in each class who are doing well. You can stay the extra hour if you like.

Juan: Well, I don't have anything else to do.

Narrator: Annie is the lifeguard during the swim hour. She walks around the pool, carefully watching each swimmer. As Juan strays into deep water, she blows her whistle as a warning.

Annie: *(Blowing her whistle)* You're not ready for that yet, Wayne!

Narrator: Juan hates having her yell at him in front of everyone else. But he tightens his lips and says nothing.

End of Act Five

Act Six

Narrator: One afternoon several weeks later, Annie surprises Juan.

Annie: Okay, hotshot. Yes, I mean you, Wayne. You think you can handle yourself in the deep water? How about swimming the length of the pool, then?

Juan: *(Suddenly afraid)* But . . . but . . . my leg!

Annie: What about your leg? Think you're the only guy who ever had a leg hurt in an accident? Have you ever heard of a guy named Franklin Roosevelt, Wayne?

Juan: *(Mumbling)* Wasn't he something in our government or in a war?

Annie: Something to do with government? He was elected president of the whole country four times, that's all! But he had two bad legs. He had to use crutches to walk, and he had to drag his legs along. Why, he even had trouble standing! But he swam! Every day of his life he swam. He didn't whine about his legs, either.

Juan: *(Angrily)* All right! All right! I'll try, but if I can't . . .

Annie: What do you think I'm the lifeguard for? I'll pull you out. *(Pauses)* Well, turkey, are you going to try or not?

Narrator: Juan wades through the shallow water to one end of the pool. He turns and glares at Annie. Then he begins to swim. The first ten meters are easy. Then his arms feel heavy, and his legs lose their kick. He gasps for breath. He thinks he'll never make it. He sees Annie walking beside him along the edge of the pool, holding a stopwatch. Juan thinks she wants him to make a fool of himself in front of all the others! Well, he'll show her! He finds new energy. It doesn't make him go any faster, but he knows he can do it now. Three strokes to go . . . then two . . . then one. He touches the other end of the pool! Annie looks down at him. She is smiling. She grabs his outstretched hand and pulls him out.

Annie: You did it, Wayne. You did it!

Juan: *(Out of breath)* Juan!

Annie: You're no chicken, and you're no turkey. I take that back. *(Looking at her stopwatch)* But 50 seconds to swim 25 meters? You're going to have to do a whole lot better than that!

Narrator: Annie walks away. Before Juan can think about her last remark, Judd Burns is slapping him on the back.

Judd: Juan, that was great! Aren't you proud of yourself?

Juan: It was okay, I guess.

End of Act Six

Act Seven

Narrator: In a few days Juan is able to swim the pool with ease. His time gets better and better. Sometimes he catches Annie looking at him with an expression of pride on her face. But when she sees that he is looking at her, too, she turns her back to him. Still, every now and then she speaks a word or two of praise.

Annie: You're getting on there, Wayne. Way to go!

Act Eight

Narrator: One morning a few days later, Juan sees Annie downtown. He is on the school bus, and she is looking in a store window. The bus stops, and Juan sticks his head out the window.

Juan: *(Yelling)* Annie! Hey, Annie!

Narrator: Annie never turns her head, even though Juan is sure she has heard him call.

Juan: *(To himself)* She thinks she's such a big deal! She can't even say hello? Just because she's a swimming champ. Is that it? Well, one of these days I'll show her!

End of Act Eight

Act Nine

Narrator: As Juan enters the locker room the next afternoon, Judd Burns stops him.

Judd: Juan, how would you like to be on the swimming team as of today?

Juan: Me? But I only learned to swim a few weeks ago, Mr. Burns. I'm not good enough yet.

Judd: *(Laughing)* That's why we want and need you . . . because you're a new swimmer, I mean. We have a beginner's event today, a 25-meter freestyle race. Annie came to me and recommended you.

Juan: *(Stunned)* Annie did?

Judd: That's right. How about it?

Juan: Annie thinks I should race? *(Pauses)* Okay, Mr. Burns, I'll race.

Narrator: Juan changes into his swimsuit quickly in the locker room and goes out to the pool area. It is packed with swimmers of all ages, and the noise they are making is deafening. He looks around until he finds Annie sitting in the bleachers with a group of girls. Lisa is with her.

Lisa: Hi, Juan. Annie tells me you're going to race today.

Juan: *(Blushing)* Yes, that's right, Lisa. *(Turning to Annie)* Thanks for picking me, Annie.

Annie: It was nothing. You make me proud, now.

Narrator: They smile at each other, and then Juan moves away. He finds a seat high in the stands where he can be alone, yet see everything.

Announcer: Okay, we need the contestants for the second race now. This is the 50-meter backstroke. Everyone into the water. Let's go. Let's go!

Narrator: Annie and the other swimmers in the 50-meter backstroke lower themselves into the water and hold on to the edge of the pool, their backs facing the far end of the pool.

Announcer: On your mark. Get set. Go! *(Sound of a gun being fired)*

Narrator: It occurs to Juan that he has never seen Annie really swim before. She is smooth and fast! When Annie makes her turn at the far end of the pool, only one other girl is even close. Neck and neck, shoulder to shoulder, Annie and her opponent race on. Then in the last five meters, Annie suddenly shoots ahead. It is as if another engine in her body has been flipped on. She finishes in first place by two full strokes.

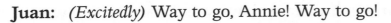

Juan: *(Excitedly)* Way to go, Annie! Way to go!

Narrator: The cheers for Too-Fast Annie shake the room as she walks back to her place in the stands. But she pays no attention. It is as if she hasn't heard a single sound.

Juan: *(To himself)* Stuck up! She could at least smile or wave at the crowd. After all, they're cheering her!

Announcer: Next race is the 25-meter freestyle. Please, contestants, take your places.

Narrator: A nervous Juan Villa takes his place on the starting block. When the gun goes off, he is momentarily frozen in place. But a clean dive and a few strong strokes bring him up to the others. Stroking furiously, Juan breaks into the lead for the first few meters. Then, challenged by the swimmer in the next lane, he seems to give way. As Juan touches the edge of the pool, a judge taps him on the shoulder and calls out, "Lane 3, second place!" Juan crawls out of the pool and finds himself facing a happy Judd Burns. Annie and Lisa come over and stand on either side of Juan.

Judd: Good job, son! You've really come along. You'll be one of our champs one day!

Annie: Champ? You're more like a chump! You know, I was right the first time, Wayne. You are a chicken. I saw you. You could have done better! You could have won! But you didn't even try to fight off that turkey in the next lane. You've got no guts!

Narrator: Annie turns away and starts to talk with Lisa. Juan sees red.

Juan: *(Yelling)* Look, I didn't even ask to be in your old race! What's with you, anyway? I wasn't too bad. Second place isn't bad. You think it's easy, do you? You think it's easy swimming with one leg?

Narrator: The crowd around them becomes silent. Everyone stares at Juan. Everyone but Annie, that is. She never even turns around. Instead she continues to talk as if she has not heard anything Juan has said to her.

Judd: Why are you yelling at Annie like that, Juan? Don't you know she can't hear you? She's deaf. Haven't you noticed she's always facing you when you talk? That's so she can read your lips.

Narrator: Juan feels like a fool. He understands everything now—why she snubbed him when he shouted at her from the bus, why she tries so hard to be the best, why she works so hard with him. Now he knows why she calls him Wayne instead of Juan. He taps her on the shoulder. Annie turns and stares at him.

Annie: What do you want?

Juan: Maybe you are right, Annie. Maybe I didn't swim as hard as I could have. I'm sorry I let you down, but wait till next time. Next time I'll win, I promise!

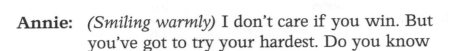

Annie: *(Smiling warmly)* I don't care if you win. But you've got to try your hardest. Do you know what I mean?

Juan: *(Smiling back)* I know . . . now. Look, I didn't know anything about your . . . about your . . .

Annie: About my being deaf? So what? When you think about it, everybody has a disability, one way or another. The point is not to let it get you down, Wayne.

Juan: *(Speaking carefully)* Juan. My name is Juan.

Annie: Your name is Juan? It's not Wayne?

Juan: That's right.

Annie: *(Laughing)* Well, what do you know about that!

End of Play

Name _____ Date _____

Juan's Story: What Do You Remember?

 Darken the letter by the correct answer.

1. How did Juan hurt his leg?
   Ⓐ in a bus accident
   Ⓑ in a softball accident
   Ⓒ in a bicycle accident
   Ⓓ in a swimming accident

2. When did Juan learn that Annie was deaf?
   Ⓐ on the first day of swimming class
   Ⓑ when Lisa asked him to umpire
   Ⓒ after his swimming race
   Ⓓ before Annie won her race

3. Juan thought Annie snubbed him when he shouted at her from the bus. What does *snubbed him* mean?
   Ⓐ hurt his toe
   Ⓑ ignored him
   Ⓒ yelled at him
   Ⓓ took his place

4. This play is mostly about how
   Ⓐ one must work hard to overcome personal problems.
   Ⓑ some people are better swimmers than others.
   Ⓒ bicycles can be dangerous.
   Ⓓ swimming is good for you.

5. You can conclude that Juan felt like a fool because
   Ⓐ Annie called him Wayne.
   Ⓑ he thought he was the only one with problems.
   Ⓒ he did not umpire the softball game.
   Ⓓ his bicycle had a flat tire.

6. When Juan races again, he will probably
   Ⓐ try harder.
   Ⓑ not try at all.
   Ⓒ hurt his leg again.
   Ⓓ wish he was playing softball.

7. What is one good quality that Juan possesses? Give an example of something he did or said to support your answer.

   _____

   _____

Juan's Story: What's That Word?

 Rewrite each sentence. Replace the underlined word or words with a synonym from the box.

disability	deafening	momentarily	altogether

1. The noise around the swimming pool was <u>very loud</u>.

   _____

2. Juan was lucky he did not lose his leg <u>completely</u>.

   _____

3. Juan was frozen <u>for a short while</u> on the starting block.

   _____

4. Juan did not know about Annie's <u>hearing problem</u>.

   _____

 Rewrite each sentence. Replace the underlined word or words with an antonym from the box.

sharp	bitterly	abruptly	tough

5. Life is <u>easy</u> for Juan.

   _____

6. Juan spoke <u>cheerfully</u> about his hurt leg.

   _____

7. Juan did not like Annie's <u>kind</u> words.

   _____

8. Juan turned <u>slowly</u> and headed for the locker room.

   _____

Juan's Story: What Do You Think?

⭐ Make a poster about bicycle safety or swimming safety. Do a sketch of your poster below. Give tips about how to be safe in the water or on a bicycle. Include a picture. When your sketch is complete, use it to make a large poster. Display your poster in the classroom.

✏️ Juan's Story: Write Away!

Choose a character from *Juan's Story* who is most like you. Write two paragraphs explaining the similarities.

Backstage

Meet the Players

Character	Reading Level
Mr. Taylor, *assistant principal*	6.0
Vendor, *a T-shirt salesperson*	5.0
Pem, *a teenaged girl*	4.5
Camika, *a teenaged girl*	4.0
Haley, *a teenaged girl*	4.0
Alex, *a teenaged boy*	2.6
Lance Britney, *a pop singer*	2.4
Guard, *a security guard*	2.0

Play Summary

Four young teens go to a concert to see a pop singer, Lance Britney. One of them, Alex, is a smart-alecky boy who likes to make fun of everything because that's how people think of him. The three girls really like Lance Britney. After the concert, they sneak backstage to meet their idol, only to discover that Lance Britney is really Chester Jenkins, a young man who is not at all like his stage persona. The girls go away from the encounter disenchanted, but Alex feels a new kinship for the singer.

Vocabulary

concert, pp. 97, 99, 103, 111
criticize, pp. 98, 99
fashion, p. 98
regret, p. 100
deranged, p. 100

consumer, p. 100
melodious, p. 102
vocal, p. 102
stylings, p. 102
guidance, p. 102
worthwhile, p. 103

concession stand, p. 103
security, pp. 105, 106, 107
fanfare, p. 108
autograph, p. 110

Tapping Prior Knowledge

Before reading the play, discuss these questions with students.

1. Have you ever been to a concert? What was it like?

2. Do you have a favorite singer or actor? What do you think that person is really like?

3. Do you think you would be the same person you are now if you suddenly became famous?

Backstage

Thinking It Over

The following questions may be used for oral discussion or as written exercises.

1. Alex criticized or made fun of people. What reason did he give for doing so?

2. Haley seems the most upset that Lance Britney is not really who she thought he was. Why do you think that is so?

3. Do you think Chester Jenkins likes being Lance Britney? Does Chester really try to fool people?

4. Why does Alex change the way he feels about Lance Britney?

Presenting the Play

Radio Play: Use these sound effects to present *Backstage* as a radio play.

• taped music to indicate act breaks—pp. 99, 103, 105, 110
• crowd noise—Act Two, pp. 99–103
• knock on door—Act Four, p. 108

Classroom Play: To stage the play in the classroom, use the sound effects listed for the radio play and the props listed below.

• T-shirts—Act Two, pp. 100–101
• stool for security guard—Act Four, pp. 106–107
• wig—Act Four, p. 108

Extending the Play

Use these activities to enrich the students' experience with readers' theater.

1. Use any or all of the blackline masters on pages 164–168.

2. Have students draw a picture of themselves as a famous pop singer.

3. Have students write a new song for Lance Britney, then sing it for the class.

4. Ask students if they ever changed their feeling about someone after getting to know that person better.

READERS' THEATER II

Presents

BACKSTAGE

LANCE BRITNEY

DRESSING ROOM

by D.W. Skrabanek

Cast

(in order of appearance)

Camika, *a teenaged girl*

Alex, *a teenaged boy*

Haley, *a teenaged girl*

Pem, *a teenaged girl*

Vendor, *a T-shirt salesperson*

Mr. Taylor, *assistant principal*

Guard, *a security guard*

Lance Britney, *a pop singer*

Act One

Camika: Hey, girlfriends. Did you hear the big news?

Alex: The moon is really made of green cheese?

Camika: No, goofball, something really important. *(She sings.)* "You broke my heart like a truck going 80, Why can't you love me, love me, baby?"

Haley: You absolutely have to be kidding.

Camika: It's true. Lance Britney is coming to town. His concert is Saturday night.

Pem: Ohh, Lance Britney. He's so dreamy. I love the way his hair is so poofy.

Haley: Mrs. Lance Britney. I can see it now. We walk down the aisle to his sweetest sweet love song, *(Singing)* "I love you forever. What's your name again?" They could film our honeymoon for MTV.

Alex: You people are goofy, because everybody knows that Lance Britney is a goose. I can probably sing better than he can.

Haley: You're just jealous.

Alex: Jealous of what, his hair dryer?

Pem: Why do you always have to be so critical?

Alex: It's my role. People expect it of me.

Camika: Well, stop it. We like Lance Britney.

Alex: He's still a goose.

Camika: You already said that.

Alex: He probably gets up each morning, puts on a mask, turns on a CD player, and starts mouthing the words. He's a toad.

Camika: I said, stop it. You just want to ruin everything for us.

Haley: Yeah, stop it. We're going to the concert.

Alex: Can I go?

Pem: You're kidding, of course.

Camika: Are you nuts? Boys don't like Lance Britney. He's too mushy, remember?

Haley: I get it. You just want to go so you can criticize Lance.

Pem: Maybe he wants some fashion tips. Can you imagine Alex with poofy hair? Oh, Alex, you're so dreamy.

Alex: No . . . no, I just thought someone should protect you from . . . uh, you know.

Camika: Sure, I'll bet. Anyway, we can take care of ourselves.

Alex: I know, I guess, but you might get lost. I can follow a trail. I was a boy scout, you know.

Pem: We can find our way.

Alex: Please, may I go?

Haley: You have to promise not to criticize Lance.

Alex: OK, I promise.

Camika: Girlfriends, what do you think?

Haley and Pem: Whatever.

Act Two

Haley: Wow, this is the first concert I've ever been to. I'm glad our parents let us come.

Alex: I'm glad they didn't come with us. Isn't that Ava and her mom over there?

Camika: I think it is.

Pem: That's so embarrassing. Isn't that Mr. Taylor, the assistant principal, over there?

Haley: It is! Be quiet. He might hear us.

Camika: What happened to his hair? It's all poofy.

Pem: It's Lance-o-mania. Everyone wants to be like Lance.

Alex: Not quite everybody. He's still a goose, you know.

Haley: He's a cute goose. Let's buy a T-shirt.

Vendor: Lance Britney T-shirts for sale right here! Get your Lance Britney T-shirts before they disappear and you regret you didn't buy one!

Haley: How much are the shirts?

Vendor: Can't you people read the sign?

Camika: What sign?

Vendor: Now where in the world did my sign go? Some deranged little brat must have stolen it. Who in their right mind would want to steal a sign?

Haley: So how much are the shirts?

Vendor: Thirty dollars each, plus tax.

Alex: You're kidding.

Vendor: No, that's the price of fame, young consumer. Do you want to purchase one, or perhaps two or three?

Pem: No way. I'm not spending thirty dollars for a stupid shirt. The ticket was already forty dollars. Does this guy think we're made of money?

Vendor: If you don't want a shirt, then move along, because other good customers are waiting. I'm just a struggling businessman trying to make an honest living.

Alex: I can see why someone stole the sign. This whole thing is just one big rip-off.

Camika: Really. Why is everything so expensive?

Alex: I guess Lance has to pay for his nine cars and four houses.

Haley: Well, I'm going to buy a shirt. Then Lance will see me in it and he'll ask me to marry him and we'll live happily ever after . . .

Alex: In his four houses?

Pem: She is goofy, isn't she?

Alex: That's what I've been saying.

Camika: Well, let's find our seats.

Pem: What about Haley?

Alex: She can float over later.

Camika: Oh, no, Mr. Taylor saw us.

Alex: Try to hide.

Pem: It's no use. He's coming this way.

Mr. Taylor: Homeboy, homegirls, what's up with the down crowd?

Camika: Mr. Taylor. Imagine meeting you here.

Mr. Taylor: Yes, well, I was just cooling . . . I mean, chilling . . . to the melodious vocal stylings of Lance Britney.

Camika: OK, well, whatever.

Alex: What happened to your hair?

Mr. Taylor: What? Oh, uh, it's a new shampoo I'm using . . . that does that.

Alex: I'd get a new shampoo if I were you.

Mr. Taylor: You realize that it's my job to say this, but I hope you kids are staying out of trouble.

Pem: We haven't had a chance to get into any yet.

Alex: And if we do meet any, your good guidance over the past few years will help us steer clear of it.

Mr. Taylor: You know, Alex, if you weren't always so concerned with being a smart aleck, you could make something worthwhile of yourself. You need to be yourself, not what you think others want you to be.

Pem: That's what we keep telling him.

Mr. Taylor: Anyway, I see my wife waving over by the concession stand. She's really the Lance Britney fan in the family. I just came along tonight to make her happy, you understand. Listen, you kids have a good time, and don't do anything I wouldn't do.

Camika and Pem: You, too, Mr. Taylor.

Pem: He's not such a bad fellow.

Alex: I don't like his attitude.

Camika: Smart Alex . . . now that's funny.

Act Three

Camika: What a great concert.

Pem: What a wonderful evening.

Haley: What a hunk.

Alex: What a bore. Not only are his songs dumb, but he can't even sing.

Haley: He most certainly can.

Alex: I don't think he was singing, because I thought I heard the CD skip once or twice.

Camika: You two stop arguing. *(Singing)* "I'm on cloud seven, Next door to heaven. Cloud seven, ooh yeah."

Pem: *(Singing)* "You broke my heart like a truck going 80, Why can't you love me, love me, baby?"

Alex: I feel like I've been hit by a truck.

Haley: You just want to make fun of others. That's because you don't know what love is. But Lance does.

Alex: OK, then, you tell me, what is love? Buying a T-shirt, getting hit by a truck?

Haley: Well, uh, Lance knows.

Alex: OK, then, let's go ask him.

Camika: What?

Alex: Let's go ask him. We'll go backstage and ask Lance personally what love is.

Pem: We can't do that.

Alex: Why not?

Pem: Well, because . . .

Haley: We weren't invited.

Alex: We'll invite ourselves.

Haley: But that's not right.

Alex: Don't you want to live on the edge? Lance would go backstage. Don't you want to be like a truck going 80?

Haley: Well, I guess so.

Camika: Uh, me too, I guess.

Pem: I'm in.

Alex: To the backstage then, ladies. After you.

Act Four

Camika: Uh, oh. Look over there.

Pem: A security guard is blocking the way. What are we going to do?

Alex: Haven't you ever heard of charm, ladies?

Pem: Not in the same breath with your name.

Alex: *(Singing)* "Oh, you stabbed my heart so deep, I think that I will go and weep."

Haley: Quit making fun of Lance's songs. We need to get backstage.

Alex: Watch true charm in action. *(To guard)* My good man, has anyone told you lately that you look like Tom Cruise?

Guard: No, and don't ask me again.

Alex: Lance Britney, perhaps?

Guard: I said no, now beat it.

Alex: Certainly George Washington.

Guard: No.

Alex: Piglet?

Guard: You kids scram right now! Don't make me get up from here. I have work to do, which you obviously didn't notice.

Alex: But, sir, I'm considering becoming a security guard. What education and job skills are required?

Guard: Well, for one thing, you have to put up with kids that bug you all the time.

Alex: I see, and what else?

Guard: You have to talk loud, so beat it, kid!

Haley: This is so not working. Alex can't get us backstage. Now I'll never meet Lance Britney.

Alex: I am not beaten yet.

Camika: We might as well go home.

Alex: Oh, sir, Mr. Security Guard.

Guard: What now?

Alex: Look over there!

Guard: Where?

Alex: Run, girls, backstage!

Guard: Hey, you kids get back here! I don't want to have to get up from here. . . . Oh, well, what harm can they do?

Alex: I told you I could get you backstage.

Haley: But where is Lance's dressing room?

Pem: It must be around here someplace.

Camika: Wait, there's a door with a star on it.

Haley: It must be the place. Lance is a bright, shining star.

Alex: Whatever you say.

Haley: So, what should we do?

Pem: Knocking would be a good start.

Haley: It seems so rude—a common knock for my Lance?

Alex: You're right. Maybe we should have a trumpet fanfare.

Camika: For once, Alex is right. Let's just knock.

(They knock on the door.)

Lance: May I help you?

Haley: *(Rather rude)* Who are you?

Lance: I'm Chester Jenkins . . . I mean, Lance Britney.

Haley: No, you're not.

Lance: Really, I'm Lance.

Haley: Lance is a lot cuter.

Alex: And he has poofier hair.

Lance: I wear a wig. It's around somewhere. And I'm not in makeup right now.

Haley: You wear a wig?

Lance: My agent didn't think my real hair looked good enough.

Camika: No way. Lance must be in another room.

Lance: I swear, I'm Lance.

Pem: Sing something.

Lance: Uh, OK. *(Singing)* "My love is like a coffee cup, and I'm waiting for you to fill it up."

Pem: You don't sound like Lance.

Lance: Oh, I have this special microphone when I sing that makes me sound better. And I have backup singers, too, you know. Singing well is not as easy as you might imagine.

Haley: I don't believe any of this. You can't be Lance Britney.

Lance: I don't know what else I can say.

Camika: What's your favorite color?

Lance: Blue.

Pem: That's what the magazine said. What's your favorite food?

Lance: Pizza.

Camika: Right again. You must be Lance Britney.

Lance: That's what I've been telling you.

Alex: Ask him what love is.

Haley: But you're nothing like the Lance Britney we know. You're supposed to be cute and sing great.

Lance: I'm just a regular guy. But my agent and the music people didn't think I was cool enough, so they made me change my name and wear a wig and sing goofy songs . . . and it worked, I guess. But sometimes I wake up in the middle of the night, and I don't even know who I am anymore. Sometimes I'm not even sure who Chester is anymore.

Alex: I know what you mean.

Lance: When I'm not performing, I'm not Lance. I guess you can't always be what people expect you to be.

Alex: I know exactly how you feel.

Lance: So, I'm sorry if I disappointed you.

Pem: It's OK. It's not your fault, really.

Lance: Would you like my autograph or something?

Haley: No, thanks.

Camika: Let's go, girls.

Alex: See you around, man.

End of Act Four

Act Five

Camika: I'm glad we're out of that place. I'll never go to another concert again.

Haley: Especially a Lance Britney concert. How could he trick us like that?

Alex: You tricked yourselves.

Camika: What do you mean?

Alex: You wanted him to be some larger-than-life, dreamy guy. And instead he's just some little toad like the rest of us.

Pem: I'm ashamed to say I agree with you. But goose, perhaps, instead of toad.

Alex: Goose it is, then. And what happened to Mrs. Chester Jenkins . . . I mean, Mrs. Lance Britney?

Haley: Oh, leave me alone.

Alex: But you know what, the strange thing is, I kind of like the guy.

Camika: What?

Alex: He reminds me of me.

Haley: You have to be kidding.

Alex: *(Singing)* "You broke my heart like a truck going 80, Why can't you love me, love me, baby?"

End of Play

Backstage: What Do You Remember?

⭐ **Darken the letter by the correct answer.**

1. What does Lance Britney do for a living?
   - Ⓐ assistant principal
   - Ⓑ T-shirt salesman
   - Ⓒ security guard
   - Ⓓ singer

2. When do Alex and the girls talk to Mr. Taylor?
   - Ⓐ before they talk to the T-shirt vendor
   - Ⓑ after they talk to the T-shirt vendor
   - Ⓒ after they talk to the security guard
   - Ⓓ after they talk to Lance Britney

3. Alex says that Lance probably puts in a CD and starts mouthing the words. What does *mouthing* mean?
   - Ⓐ acting as if he's singing the words
   - Ⓑ whistling
   - Ⓒ making rude comments
   - Ⓓ keeping his mouth closed

4. This play is mostly about how
   - Ⓐ T-shirts cost too much.
   - Ⓑ assistant principals should not go to concerts.
   - Ⓒ people often have trouble living up to others' expectations.
   - Ⓓ singers should not wear wigs.

5. Why do you think Haley was disappointed when she met Lance?
   - Ⓐ He didn't like her T-shirt.
   - Ⓑ He made fun of Alex.
   - Ⓒ He didn't ask her to get married.
   - Ⓓ He wasn't what she expected.

6. The next time Lance Britney has a concert, Haley and Camika
   - Ⓐ will probably go.
   - Ⓑ will probably not go.
   - Ⓒ will buy ten T-shirts.
   - Ⓓ will ask Lance to the school dance.

7. Why does Alex say that Lance reminds Alex of himself?

   _____

   _____

   _____

Backstage: What's That Word?

⭐ **Choose a vocabulary word from the box to complete each sentence. Write the word on the line.**

concert	regret	guidance	vocal	security	concession
fashion	autograph	deranged	consumer	melodious	criticize

1. A person who buys things is a _____.

2. An adult told the young people the right way to do things. The adult was giving

   _____.

3. Leslie drew pictures of dresses. She wanted to be a _____ designer.

4. Alex said unkind things about Lance. Haley told Alex not to

   _____ Lance.

5. A musical performance is also called a _____.

6. A person who is wild and crazy is _____.

7. Music that has a pleasant sound is _____.

8. _____ means dealing with the voice.

9. Another word for *safety* is _____.

10. People can buy food and drinks at a _____ stand.

11. The valued signature of a famous person is an _____.

12. To have bad feelings about doing something is to _____ it.

⭐ **Write a synonym and antonym for each word.**

	Synonym	**Antonym**
13. deranged	_____	_____
14. worthwhile	_____	_____
15. consumer	_____	_____
16. melodious	_____	_____

Backstage: What Do You Think?

Going to a concert can be expensive. Often, tickets, souvenirs, and refreshments have high prices.

★ **Solve the problems.**

1. Alex, Camika, Haley, and Pem each paid $40 for a concert ticket. What was the total cost for the four tickets?

   _____

2. If 2,750 people each paid $40 for a ticket, what was the total cost of tickets sold for the concert?

   _____

3. Lance Britney gets 15% of the money from ticket sales. If 2,750 people each paid $40 for a ticket, how much did Lance make?

   _____

4. The T-shirt vendor sold shirts for $30 each. He paid $12.35 for each shirt. The difference was his profit. If he sold 145 shirts, what would his total profit be?

   _____

5. Mr. Taylor bought two tickets at $40 each, a T-shirt for $30, a program for $8.75, a Lance Britney CD for $17.50, and two drinks for $3.15 each. What was the total cost of Mr. Taylor's evening at the concert?

   _____

 Backstage: Write Away!

Have you ever had expectations that another person could not meet? How did you feel when the person failed to meet your expectations? Write a paragraph or two about your experience. Use the graphic organizer to develop your ideas.

Your expectations	Your feelings

Confusion in Clone City

Meet the Players

Character	Reading Level
Narrator	6.0
Sam Shovel, *private eye*	4.0
Trent, *a young man*	2.2
Trent 2, *Trent's clone*	2.0
Trixi, *a young woman*	2.0
Trixi 2, *Trixi's clone*	2.1
Professor I.M. Nutz, *mad scientist*	4.0
Door, *a door clone in Sam's office*	2.4
Fly, *a fly clone*	2.0
Wall, *a clone at Nutz's lab*	2.1
Mosquito, *a cloned soldier insect*	2.5
Nutz 2, *Nutz's clone*	5.0
Sam 2, *Sam's clone*	4.0

Play Summary

Private eye Sam Shovel is minding his own business until two young couples ask for his help in solving a case. A mad scientist is cloning people, often without their knowledge, in an attempt to create chaos and take over the world. A comedy of errors finally leads to Sam's capture of the mad Professor Nutz and an apparent return to normality.

Vocabulary

normal, pp. 119, 135
original, p. 120
unhinged, p. 121
identity, p. 124
crisis, p. 124

chaos, p. 125
situation, p. 127
caution, p. 127
mission, p. 129
insane, p. 129

trespassing, p. 130
illegal, p. 130
unleash, p. 131
creations, p. 132
counselor, p. 133

Tapping Prior Knowledge

Before reading the play, discuss these questions with students.

1. Have you read or heard about cloning? What are your opinions on cloning animals or humans?

2. Have you ever known someone who was very like you? What about that person made him or her similar to you?

3. Have you ever wished that animals or things could talk? What do you think they would say?

Confusion in Clone City

Thinking It Over

The following questions may be used for oral discussion or as written exercises.

1. Why did Sam not seem surprised when the fly talked to him?

2. Why was Trent's clone surprised when Sam knew what he was going to say?

3. Why was the narrator surprised when the door talked to him?

4. Why did Professor Nutz create the Mosquito Men?

5. How did Sam fool Professor Nutz's clone?

Presenting the Play

Radio Play: Use these sound effects to present *Confusion in Clone City* as a radio play.

- taped music to indicate act breaks— pp. 126, 128
- fly buzzing—Act One, pp. 119, 126
- door opening—Act One, pp. 120, 122
- mosquito buzzing—Act Two, p. 128; Act Three, pp. 130, 131

Classroom Play: To stage the play in the classroom, use the sound effects listed for the radio play and the props listed below.

- name tags to distinguish the characters from their clones
- Sam's sign—Act One, pp. 119, 121
- rubber bands—Act One, p. 119
- desk and chairs for Sam's office— Act One, pp. 119–126
- laboratory equipment—Act Three, p. 128–135
- chairs to represent Sam's bed— Act Three, p. 135

Extending the Play

Use these activities to enrich the students' reading of *Confusion in Clone City.*

1. Use any or all of the blackline masters on pages 164–168.

2. Ask the students if they know their hat sizes. How do they know they are who they are?

3. Discuss puns as wordplay. Often, homophones or homographs are used in puns. Have students find the puns spoken by Door and Wall.

4. Ask students if they would like to have a clone. What would they do with a clone?

READERS' THEATER II

Presents

Confusion in Clone City

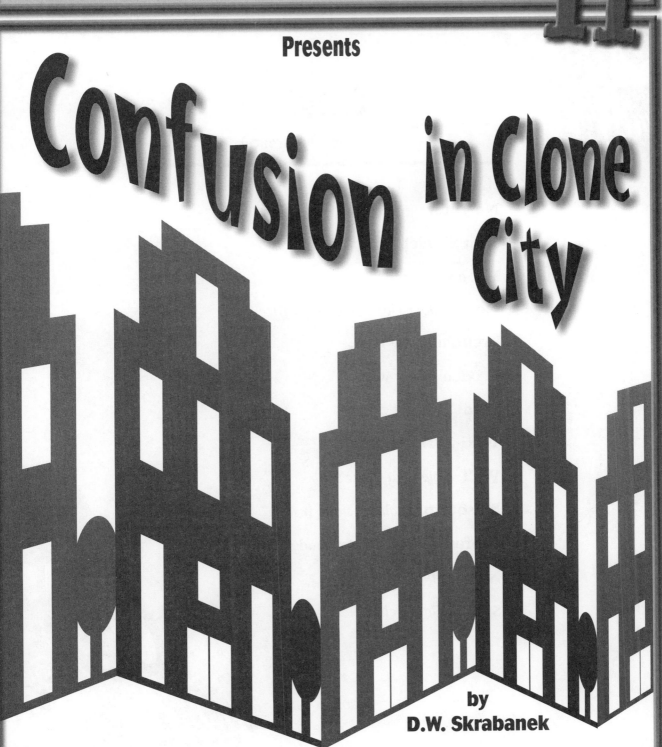

by
D.W. Skrabanek

Cast

(in order of appearance)

Narrator

Sam Shovel, *private eye*

Fly, *a fly clone*

Door, *a door clone in Sam's office*

Trent, *a young man*

Trixi, *a young woman*

Trent 2, *Trent's clone*

Trixi 2, *Trixi's clone*

Wall, *a clone at Nutz's lab*

Mosquito, *a soldier clone insect*

Professor I.M. Nutz, *mad scientist*

Nutz 2, *Nutz's clone*

Sam 2, *Sam's clone*

Act One

Narrator: It was a normal day in the office of Private Eye Sam Shovel. Which means nothing was happening. Sam dusted off his sign that said, "Sam Spade—I dig up clues." Then he put it back. Then he picked it up again. Then he put it back. After a while, Sam got really bored, so he started shooting rubber bands at a fly. And that's when things began to pick up.

Sam: Darn, just missed.

Fly: Missed, huh? I'll miss that leg you just knocked off.

Sam: Oh, sorry.

Fly: What did you expect? You were shooting rubber bands at me.

Sam: I said I was sorry.

Fly: So, you wouldn't mind if I shot rubber bands at you?

Sam: Beat it, or I'll pull out the flyswatter.

Fly: Nyah, nyah! I'm out of here. Buzzzz!

Sam: Dumb fly.

Narrator: Perhaps I failed to mention one unusual thing about Clone City. Most everyone had a clone—I think I noted that. And most every clone looked like the original. But there were exceptions—little accidents, you might say. And there was a mad scientist—Professor I.M. Nutz—who was turning out some bad clones. The fly, I believe, was the mad professor's work. And, unfortunately, there were even worse examples. But enough explanation. Suddenly, a young man and woman burst through Sam Spade's door.

Door: Hey, watch it, bud! Just who do you think you're pushing around?

Narrator: As I mentioned.

Trent: Oh, I beg your pardon.

Door: Well, OK, but don't let it happen again.

Trent: I may have to leave.

Door: Then ask.

Trent: OK.

Sam: Don't mind that door. He has mood swings all day long.

Door: Do not.

Sam: I knew I should have left you at the lumberyard.

Trixi: Please! We have a problem here.

Sam: Dumb door.

Door: I wish I could leave like the fly. Just zoom off happy as a lark. But no, I have to hang around here all day and all night.

Trixi: We need help!

Sam: What seems to be the trouble?

Trent and Trixi: We're in love.

Sam: That's good to know. But that's not my line of work.

Trent: No, we want to get married.

Sam: Then you need to go to a church. Didn't you see my sign? I'm a private eye.

Trent: No, someone is trying to break us up.

Sam: Nosy relatives, huh?

Trixi: We don't know who it is.

Trent: We'll arrange a date. Then before I arrive to pick up Trixi, some other guy will show up.

Sam: And so she goes on a date with another guy?

Trixi: No, that's not the problem. I don't want to date other guys. I love Trent.

Trent: And I love Trixi.

Door: Oh, gag. I'm getting rather unhinged here.

Sam: The door is right. Save all that stuff for the honeymoon. Back to the problem.

Trixi: The problem is that the other guy looks like Trent. Just like him.

Trent: And I feel that Trixi isn't really Trixi sometimes.

Sam: So, you're suggesting your problem is . . .

Trent and Trixi: Clones!

Narrator: Just then, another young man and woman burst through the door. They look just like Trent and Trixi.

Door: Hey, watch it, bud! Just who do you think . . . . Oh, never mind.

Trent 2: Please, we have a problem here!

Sam: I'll say. What seems to be the trouble?

Trent 2 and Trixi 2: We're in love!

Door: Oh, my gosh! They're worse than the first ones.

Sam: Shut it, door.

Trixi: It isn't open.

Trent 2: No, we want to get married!

Sam: Somehow I could have guessed that. And someone is trying to break you up.

Trent 2: That's right. Wait a minute, how did you know that?

Narrator: Suddenly, Trent finally notices Trent, and Trixi sees Trixi, and they all look a bit confused.

Trent: Say, who are you anyway?

Trent 2: Well, I'm me, of course. Or more correctly, I might be you.

Trent: No, you're not.

Trent 2: Yes, I am. And just who are you?

Trent: Well, me, of course . . . or you . . . or me.

Trent 2: See, you're not me. You're not even you.

Trent: I am, too.

Trent 2: Then prove it.

Trent: How?

Trent 2: What's your hat size?

Trent: Well, I don't know.

Trent 2: Ah-ha!

Trent: That doesn't mean anything.

Sam: It is rather convincing.

Trent: But I'm sure I'm me.

Trixi: Just who is who? Who am I supposed to marry?

Narrator: Trixi looks uncertainly at Trent, then at Trent. Meanwhile, Trixi is giving Trixi the evil eye. Goodness, this is confusing, isn't it?

Trixi: I say again, who, who am I going to marry?

Door: Is there an owl in here?

Trent and Trent 2: Marry me, me.

Trixi 2: Wait a minute. If you're both marrying her, who's marrying me?

Trent and Trent 2: Me, me.

Sam: I think there are laws against such things.

Trixi: *(To Trixi 2)* I don't like your looks, sister.

Trixi 2: I could say the same thing, but it seems a bit selfish.

Sam: OK, we seem to have an identity crisis here.

Narrator: Sam stares at Trent and Trent and Trixi and Trixi, who all stare at each other.

Door: *(To Narrator)* What did you say? You need to speak up.

Narrator: You're <u>not supposed</u> to hear me. I'm the narrator. The characters can't hear the narrator.

Door: Well, I'm maple to hear you.

Narrator: Oh, no. A door that tells puns.

Door: Don't knock it if you haven't tried it.

Narrator: You're just a troublemaker.

Door: At least I'm not ajar. And for your information, people a-door me.

Sam: Excuse me, but can we get on with it? We have serious problems here.

Narrator: Don't we all? So, anyway, Trixi is shooting eye-daggers at Trixi, and Trent is scowling at Trent, and Sam is annoying . . .

Sam: Hey!

Narrator: And the door, well, the door—

Trixi: But who could make such a terrible plan? Who would want to clone me?

Sam: You have a point. But let's review. You all did not order a clone. The clone claims to be you, but at the same time, you may be claiming to be the clone—I don't know. Someone is just creating chaos. Who could it be? Who? Who?

Door: There's that owl again.

Narrator: My guess would be the mad scientist I.M. Nutz.

Door: I thought the narrator was supposed to <u>know</u> everything.

Narrator: Maybe I do, but I'm just not telling.

Sam: Well, personally, I'd say that's a good guess. Nutz <u>is</u> nuts.

Door: I'd say it's an open and shut case.

Trent: So how do we solve it all?

Trixi: Yes, how, how?

Door: The owl is talking backwards.

Trixi: Not knowing if I'm me frightens me.

Trent 2: How do we find this mad scientist?

Sam: The phone book says his secret laboratory is at 321 Wacko Way.

Trixi 2: You are such a good detective.

Sam: You're right! I suggest we all meet at Professor Nutz's lab as soon as possible. We'll get to the bottom of this. Let's go.

Door: Well, I'm glad they're all gone. Now I can get a little peace and quiet.

Fly: Buzzzz! I'm back! Did you miss me?

Door: Not really. Why don't you play like a tree and leave?

End of Act One

Act Two

Narrator: We are all in front of the mad scientist's laboratory right now—Sam Shovel, Trent and Trent, Trixi and Trixi. Fortunately, they let me come along. Otherwise, you wouldn't know half of what's going on.

On the way over here, Sam suddenly remembered that he had met this Professor Nutz before—in the Great Confusion of Peanut Butter History case. Nutz had tried to make peanut butter without peanuts, and everyone who ate it turned into onions. It was a stinky situation. So Sam knew that Nutz was a dangerous fellow.

Sam: Now, this Professor Nutz is a dangerous fellow.

Trent: That sounds familiar.

Sam: I've tried to catch him before.

Trixi and Trixi 2: We know, we know. Just move on.

Sam: We need to proceed with caution. I feel a bit uneasy around here. I'm reminded of that old saying, "The walls have eyes."

Wall: That's a lie. But we do have ears. In fact, I'm "wall" ears.

Trent 2: His puns are worse than the door's.

Wall: I heard that.

Sam: Let's find a way inside the lab.

Trixi: That looks like a door.

Narrator: We all move that way.

Sam: This cloning stuff is too weird. You can't tell real from fake. Everything seems to be a clone.

Mosquito: That's right. And mosquito clones are the worst. We heard what you did to our fly buddy.

Sam: I didn't mean to.

Mosquito: That's what they all say. Let's get them, boys!

Trixi and Trixi 2: Do something.

Sam: Let's get out of here!

Act Three

Narrator: We were able to escape the mosquitos. Then we found a partly open window. We all scrambled through it, so now we're inside Professor Nutz's laboratory.

Sam: So now we're inside Professor Nutz's laboratory.

Narrator: I just said that.

Trixi: Would you two please hush?

Trent: That's right. We're on a mission here.

Trixi 2: Yeah, we want to get married, remember?

Sam: Well, I didn't start it.

Trent 2: Uh, hmm. We just want to marry the right person—not a clone.

Trent: Hey, you're the clone, not me.

Sam: I thought we had business here.

Nutz: That's right. I believe you are looking for me.

Narrator: In case you missed it, Professor Nutz suddenly appeared.

Trixi: Why are you so angry, Professor?

Nutz: I'm not angry mad, I'm insane mad. Or at least that's what the media says. Personally, I think I'm a nice guy.

Sam: Don't try to change the subject, Nutz. I know how sneaky you are.

Nutz: And I know what a great private eye you are. Let me see if I remember correctly. You didn't catch me the last time, either.

Sam: There's a good reason for that.

Nutz: Which is?

Sam: I'll have to think of one. But you're trying to change the subject again. You're under arrest, Nutz.

Nutz: I'm under arrest? You're the one that's trespassing.

Narrator: That is a good point.

Mosquito: There they are, boys! Attack!

Trent: The mosquitos again! Who left the window open? Ow! Ow!

Nutz: At ease, Mosquito Men.

Mosquito: Aw, shucks!

Sam: Friends of yours?

Nutz: My troops, actually. For when I take over the world. I cloned a bunch of the best soldiers and made them even better.

Sam: You are mad. And as I mentioned before, you're under arrest.

Nutz: You never did say why.

Sam: OK, well, for illegal cloning.

Nutz: This is Clone City. That's what people do here—they clone.

Sam: Well, then, for trying to take over the world.

Nutz: But I haven't started to take over the world . . . yet.

Narrator: Another good point. For those keeping score, Professor Nutz seems to have more good points than Sam Shovel.

Sam: Doesn't matter. You're headed to the Big House, Nutz. But first, I'm taking you downtown for questioning.

Nutz: Perhaps you are forgetting my Mosquito Men. I have you surrounded.

Narrator: Another good point.

Sam: Oh, hush! Let me think.

Nutz: What's to think about? Either you surrender or I unleash the Mosquito Men on you. What will it be?

Sam: Well, I guess you have me again, Nutz. Let's . . . get them, boys! Slap!

Mosquito: Buzz! Eee!

Trent and Trent 2: Slap, slap!

Trixi and Trixi 2: Slap, slap, slap!

Mosquito: Buzz! Eee!

Narrator: I'm just the narrator. I'm a reporter, not a fighter.

Sam: Slap, slap!

Mosquito: Buzz! Ee! Buzzzzzzz . . . *(Fades)*

Sam: So much for the Mosquito Men.

Nutz: My marvelous creations! What have you done?

Sam: You should ask yourself the same question. You know what can happen when you fool with science.

Nutz: All I wanted was to rule the world. What's wrong with that?

Sam: People don't like to be ruled—not by Mosquito Men or mad scientists—not by anything. They like to live in freedom and peace. So you've failed again, you crazy mad scientist. And this time I have you at last.

Nutz: Not so fast, Shovel. That would be too easy. I'm not really Professor Nutz. I'm his clone.

Sam: No way.

Narrator: Another interesting twist.

Nutz 2: *(Entering)* He's right. I'm really Nutz.

Sam: I don't believe it.

Nutz 2: It's true.

Sam: Then tell me a joke.

Nutz 2: What?

Sam: Tell me a joke.

Nutz 2: I'm a clone, not a clown . . . oops.

Sam: Ah-ha!

Nutz: Dumb clone. Curses, foiled again.

Sam: Let's go, Nutz. I really have you this time.

Narrator: And so Sam Shovel saves the day.

Trent and Trent 2, Trixi and Trixi 2: Wait a minute. What about us?

Sam: What about you?

Trent and Trent 2, Trixi and Trixi 2: Whom should we marry?

Sam: Well, I'm no marriage counselor, but in the land of the free and the home of the brave, you can usually marry anybody you choose to . . . and I guess the same holds true in Clone City.

Trixi: *(To Trent 2)* Then I want to marry this Trent.

Trent: Trixi!

Trent 2: I have to admit. I am a clone.

Trixi: Well, I've decided you're a lot better than the real thing.

Trent: Trixi!

Trent 2: I'm flattered. Well, then, will you marry me?

Trixi: Yes, yes, yes.

Sam: OK, so that's settled. Let's go, Nutz.

Trent: Wait, what about me? This was all my idea in the first place.

Sam: OK, I'll send the bill to you.

Trent: No, whom will I marry?

Sam: I don't know. Why are there always all these loose ends to tie up? Listen, there must be millions of girls and clones out there to choose from. Just go find one.

Trent: But I wanted Trixi. We were in love.

Sam: OK, if you say so.

Trixi 2: I'm almost Trixi, and if she loved you, I probably do, but I'm not really sure . . . but I'll marry you, I guess.

Trent: Well, OK. I guess that's better than nothing.

Narrator: And true love triumphs again. And justice triumphs again. And order triumphs again. The moral of all this is, I suppose, that cloning can be very confusing, if nothing else. But now, everything is in its place once more, and we can all go home.

Sam 2: Well, not quite.

Narrator: Who are you?

Sam 2: I am Sam Shovel, famous private eye.

Sam: No, you're not. I'm Sam Shovel, famous private eye.

Sam 2: I beg to differ.

Sam: It's simple. You are not me.

Sam 2: Prove it. What's your hat size?

Sam: I don't know.

Sam 2: Ah-ha!

Sam: Aieeee!

Narrator: *(Almost whispering)* Suddenly, Sam awoke from his frightful dream. He rubbed his tired eyes and looked sleepily around the dim bedroom.

Sam: What a weird dream. Man, oh, man, am I glad to be safe in my own bed.

Narrator: So all does return to normal in Clone City . . . or does it? It was all a dream . . . or was it?

Sam: Hey, who are you? What are you doing in here?

Narrator: Uh, nothing.

End of Play

Confusion in Clone City: What Do You Remember?

⭐ **Darken the letter by the correct answer.**

1. What was Sam Shovel's job?
   Ⓐ narrator
   Ⓑ mad scientist
   Ⓒ private eye
   Ⓓ ditch digger

2. When did Sam meet his own clone?
   Ⓐ when Trent and Trixi came to his office
   Ⓑ after he arrested Professor Nutz
   Ⓒ before the mosquito attacked him
   Ⓓ after he woke up from his dream

3. At the end, the narrator says that true love triumphs. What does *triumphs* mean?
   Ⓐ wins
   Ⓑ loses
   Ⓒ turns into a clone
   Ⓓ goes to jail

4. This play is mostly about how
   Ⓐ all scientists are mad.
   Ⓑ doors are noisy.
   Ⓒ you should be kind to flies.
   Ⓓ cloning can cause confusion.

5. You can conclude that
   Ⓐ Professor Nutz escaped again.
   Ⓑ Sam may have dreamed the whole thing.
   Ⓒ doors and walls really can talk.
   Ⓓ everyone should have a clone.

6. If Sam is offered another case about clones, he will probably
   Ⓐ become a mad scientist.
   Ⓑ get a new door.
   Ⓒ not take it.
   Ⓓ buy a bigger flyswatter.

7. Sam tells Nutz, "You know what can happen when you fool with science." What does Sam mean?

   _____

   _____

   _____

Confusion in Clone City: What's That Word?

★ Use vocabulary words from the box to complete the puzzle

normal

original

chaos

caution

mission

insane

trespassing

illegal

unleash

Across

1. when things are out of control

5. a task or goal

8. going on someone's property without permission

9. against the law

Down

2. the real thing; not a copy

3. a warning or extra carefulness

4. release or let go

6. ordinary or average

7. crazy; not reasonable

Confusion in Clone City: What Do You Think?

⭐ Think about having a clone of yourself as your best friend. Consider your good qualities and traits. Then, list at least seven of these qualities or traits you would want your clone to have. Finally, write a short play in which you and your clone discuss a problem. Include how the problem is solved. Use another piece of paper to write your play.

1. _____

2. _____

3. _____

4. _____

5. _____

6. _____

7. _____

✏️ Confusion in Clone City: Write Away!

Cloning is often in the news. Some scientists want to clone humans. What do you think? Should humans be cloned? What problems might happen if humans were cloned? Write a persuasive paragraph telling why humans should or should not be cloned. Use the graphic organizer to develop your ideas.

Why humans should be cloned	Why humans should not be cloned

Meet the Players

Character	Reading Level
Pecos Bill, *a cowboy*	3.0
John Henry, *a railroad worker*	4.2
Calamity Jane, *a woman of the Old West*	3.6
Paul Bunyan, *a lumberjack*	2.9
Sally Ann Thunder Ann Whirlwind, *a woman of the Eastern frontier*	3.2
Coyote, *a Native American spirit*	3.1
Slue-Foot Sue, *a cowgirl*	3.7
Announcer	5.5
Referee	2.5

Note: Unlike the other plays in this book, which use an everyday form of conversation, this play emphasizes the genre of storytelling. As a result, many of the speeches reflect the flow of narration, and the sentence structure reflects the ongoing nature of the action. Such a reading exercise gives students additional practice in verbal fluency.

Play Summary

The first annual Showdown at the Not-So-OK Corral features some of the most ornery tale-twisters you would ever want to hear. A colorful array of tall-tale and legendary characters spin yarns amid boasting and good-natured ribbing. Though the threats of "whupping" one another are numerous, the play ends on a didactic note as the characters retire to discuss their differences over a cup of sassafras tea.

Vocabulary

contestants, p. 143   *penalty*, p. 146   *contraption*, p. 153
participants, p. 143   *ornery*, p. 147   *recollect*, p. 154
prefer, p. 145   *galluses*, p. 147   *recall*, p. 154
abiding, p. 146   *plague*, p. 148   *buzzard*, p. 155
traditions, p. 146   *floundering*, p. 151   *honorary*, p. 156

Teacher Notes

Tapping Prior Knowledge

Before reading the play, discuss these questions with students.

1. Describe how you feel about people who brag a lot.

2. Do you have a relative who is the storyteller of the family? What do you like or dislike about your family's stories?

3. Have you read stories or seen shows about any of the characters in the play? Which character is your favorite?

Thinking It Over

The following questions may be used for oral discussion or as written exercises.

1. One key feature of a tall tale is exaggeration. How is Sally Ann Thunder Ann Whirlwind's story exaggerated? How is Slue-Foot Sue's story exaggerated?

2. Coyote is a Native American character. He says that his people were one with the Earth. What does that mean? How does his story illustrate that idea?

3. Which character do you think should win the showdown?

Presenting the Play

Radio Play: Use these sound effects to present *Showdown at the Not-So-OK Corral* as a radio play.

- a bell to indicate round breaks—pp. 145, 151, 158
- crowd noise—beginnings of rounds, pp. 143, 146, 152, 159
- sounds of storm—Round Two, p. 147
- sounds of battle—Round Two, p. 148
- fish tail splashing—Round Two, p. 150
- ax chopping tree—Round Three, p. 152
- shotgun firing—Round Three, p. 152
- hammering, clanking, and banging—Round Three, p. 153
- rain falling, water roaring—Round Three, p. 155
- tornado—Round Three, p. 157

Classroom Play: To stage the play in the classroom, use the sound effects listed for the radio play and the props listed below.

- microphone for Announcer—pp. 143, 148, 149
- stools for the contestants in the showdown
- assorted clothes and items appropriate to each character: whip, lasso, ax, sledgehammer, cowboy hats, etc.

Extending the Play

Use these activities to enrich the students' reading of the play.

1. Use any or all of the blackline masters on pages 164–168.

2. Many of the characters use colloquial language in the play. Colloquial language is a conversational form of speech often peculiar to a certain time or region. For example, all the characters talk about "whupping" each other. *Whup* means to "whip" or "beat up." Have the students locate other bits of colloquial language in the play or have them listen for colloquial language in their everyday conversations.

3. Many characters mention specific geographical locations in the play. Have students locate these places on a map.

Teacher Notes

READERS' THEATER II

Presents

SHOWDOWN AT THE NOT-SO-OK CORRAL

by D.W. Skrabanek

Cast

(in order of appearance)

Announcer

Pecos Bill, *a cowboy*

John Henry, *a railroad worker*

Calamity Jane, *a woman of the Old West*

Paul Bunyan, *a lumberjack*

Sally Ann Thunder Ann Whirlwind, *a woman of the Eastern frontier*

Referee

Coyote, *a Native American spirit*

Slue-Foot Sue, *a cowgirl*

Round One

Announcer: To our listening audience, and to all the ships at sea, good evening, and welcome to the first annual Showdown at the Not-So-OK Corral. We are here at ringside, breathlessly awaiting the arrival of your contestants. We have a full slate for the evening, ladies and gentlemen. You will be crazed and amazed by the zingers we will hear tonight. Oh, wait, I believe some of the participants are approaching. One moment, please.

Bill: Yeehaw! I feel good tonight. This will be over soon. Yeehaw!

John: You're right about that, cowboy. And I thank you for the early congratulations.

Bill: I wasn't talking about you. I was talking about me. I aim to win this here showdown.

Jane: I heard you were a card, Bill, a real wiseacre. And what you just said was mighty funny. I'll be the last one standing, or my name isn't Calamity Jane. You know that I can do anything you can . . . only better.

Bill: My spurs are trembling in fright, you can bet.

Paul: They should be, because you little runts don't stand a chance against a real man— a lumberjack—like me.

Sally: Say, aren't you that Paul Bunyan feller?

Paul: That's right.

Sally: I heard of you. You like pancakes or something, so I hear.

Bill: How are you going to win, Bunyan? Gag us with that stinky miscolored cow of yours?

Paul: Listen, Pecos Bill . . .

Bill: It's Pecos William to you.

Paul: Listen, you. Babe is not a cow. He's an ox, a blue ox.

Bill: Oooh, Babe. Tough name. My Widowmaker could take that cow of yours with one leg tied behind his mane.

Paul: You take that back or I'll whup you.

Bill: Never happen.

Sally: I don't know, Bill. He's a big one. And I whupped you several times myself.

Bill: Never happened.

Referee: Settle down, people. We don't want a ruckus before the showdown begins. Save it for later.

Sally: Aw, you take the fun out of everything.

Referee: Just my job, mam. Now, is everybody here?

John: Who's that slinking around over yonder?

Referee: *(Calling)* Coyote, get your tail over here. Join the group. Come on.

Coyote: I prefer the old ways.

Referee: That's fine, too. And you can get back to those old ways sooner if you come on over here quicker.

Coyote: If you insist.

Referee: I do. Now, who else is missing? Bill, any ideas on Slue-Foot Sue?

Bill: Still bouncing.

Referee: Well, we'll have to get started without her.

Bill: All-righty, I reckon that's how it's got to be.

Referee: Good. Now, you all know the rules. No cussin', no ear-bitin', and no shootin' during the showdown. We want to do this in a friendly manner. All agreed?

All: *(Reluctantly)* Yeah.

Referee: Then come out talking, and may the best man or woman win.

Bill: Yeehaw! Let's go! Yeehaw!

End of Round One

Round Two

Referee: I guess we should get this show on the road, then. I don't think we can be waiting for Sue anymore, Bill.

Bill: That's fine. She may drop in anyway.

Referee: In the interest of being civil and abiding by the Tall-Tale Teller Table of Traditions, then, ladies first.

Jane: Go ahead, Sally Ann.

Sally: Why, thank you kindly, Calamity. When I was born . . .

Paul: When I was born, I weighed 80 pounds.

Referee: One penalty point against Paul Bunyan.

Bill: Give that stinky cow a penalty point, too.

Sally: Actually, that might be my skunk perfume, Bill.

Referee: Order! Now, go on, Sally Ann.

Sally: As I was saying, before I was so rudely interrupted—

Paul: Sorry.

Sally: When I was born, I was already an ornery little critter. I looked around and saw my nine brothers, and I yelled so loud it'd knock the ears off a jackrabbit, "My name is Sally Ann Thunder Ann Whirlwind!" And they looked at me kind of dumb and said, "You can't talk." And I said, "Maybe not, but I can out-yell and out-run any little old baby in all of Kentuck. And I reckon I can do the same to you." And they said, "Babies can't run." And I said, "Maybe so." And then we tore off up the path, me ahead and those nine boys huffing and puffing behind. And when we got to the end of the path, well, I didn't stop. I just lit out for the woods, faster than lickety-split, where I stayed until I was eight. When I finally came home, I had a lasso of six rattlesnakes on my belt and a grizzly bear over my shoulder.

(The others give her mild applause.)

Referee: All right, then. Now we move on to Calamity Jane.

Jane: Well, I'm afraid mine pales next to that. I was a regular gal till I was 10, though they tell me I could ride a wild mustang before I could talk. After my dear mama died, we headed west to Nevadee, and when a storm rose up, lightning flashing and thunder crashing, I was split up from my papa and my brothers. I was in the world all alone. By the time I was 20, I was wearing men's clothes, galluses and all, and I

was a head army scout. Lots of folks, even men, called me the most daring rider and the best shot in all the western country. About that time, I rode smack dab into the middle of a battle, with screaming and shooting all around me. I plucked up a Captain Egan and plopped him down on the horse right in front of me, and then I carried him the last four miles back to the fort. Finally we reached the fort, and Captain Egan, who was bleeding bad from his wounds and must have been out of his head, he said, "Miss Canary—" That was my real name, Martha Jane Canary. He said, "—I name you Calamity Jane, the heroine of the plains." And that there is how I got my name.

Coyote: My people called her the White Devil of the Yellowstone.

Jane: I did not start the smallpox, my coyote friend, and I'm sorry for what it did to your people. I only know I helped to nurse the sick in Deadwood during that plague.

Referee: Well, I guess we'll move on to the gentlemen.

Announcer: Suddenly there is a loud noise from above, and then in a rush of ruffles and hoops and with a loud *PLOING!*, Slue-Foot Sue lands feet first in the middle of the showdown.

Sue: I do believe it's my turn.

Bill: Sue, sweetheart, I ain't seen you in a month of Sundays.

Sue: Durn right. You knew that mangy mule of yours would throw me.

Bill: I tried to warn you. I told you not to get on Widowmaker. But you was too highfalutin and cocky, and you made me let you, so when he threw you and you bounced in that big old hoop skirt, it was the funniest thing I had ever seen. Then you bounced again, *(His head bobs.)* and again, higher and higher. And purty soon, there wasn't nothing I could do.

Sue: So you tried to shoot me?

Bill: It seemed like a good idea at the time. I thought you might be starving.

Sue: So you tried to shoot me! I guess I'm lucky you're a bad shot.

Bill: My aim is true. Maybe I missed on purpose. Maybe I didn't want to lose my wife right after my wedding day. Still, it wasn't my fault you bounced up to the moon and back down to Earth, *(Head bobbing)* up and down, up and down, up and down, up and . . . all those years.

Sue: We will discuss the matter later. I have some yarn-spinning to do right now.

Referee: Ladies and gentlemen, Slue-Foot Sue.

Sue: Thanks very much. Now, I do not mean to bore you to tears with dreary tales of my childhood— as these other ladies have done.

(Jane and Sally hiss at her.)

Sue: *(To Sally)* You stay away from my man, Sally Ann, or I'll whup you.

Sally: You can have him. He's kind of puny anyway, compared to my Davy.

Sue: Well, consider yourself warned. And you stay away too, Calam.

Jane: My heart is pining only for Wild Bill, not your Bill.

Sue: Keep it that way. Now, when I was a younger woman—not to say I ain't young now, but traveling ages you—I was a big old gal who could do the work of ten men—easy. Even ten Bunyans.

Paul: Funny.

Sue: It was a hot Texas day, hot as all git out, and I felt like being wild, so I put my two little fingers between my lips and whistled so loud the folks in New Mexico thought a train was coming. And right out of the Rio Grande, which is where I was, popped this big old catfish, big as a whale he was, and I yelled, "Yeehaw!" and that big old catfish slapped his tail so hard it knocked plumb all the water out of that river. And while he was

there floundering around in that muddy puddle, I grabbed him round the neck and wrassled him to a standstill. Then I climbed on his back, waving my lasso and shooting my six-gun so fast the clouds were punched full of holes and the rain poured out and filled up that river again. We took off down the river, that old big fish trying to buck me off and me hanging on tighter than a flea on a rat's ear. And as we came round a bend, I saw this big old cowboy up on the bluff and I yelled "Howdy!" and he yelled "Howdy!" and that was the first time I saw Bill, and it was true love. So I jumped ashore and that fish went on to fight Captain Ahab or somebody, and Bill proposed to me that very day, and the next day we was married, and to make a long story short, to show me how much he loved me, he let me ride that mangy horse Widowmaker, and I been bouncing around ever since. And that's my story.

Sally: Can we wake up now?

Sue: You just hush.

End of Round Two

Round Three

Referee: Well, that's it for the ladies. Now we move on to the men. We have a far piece to go yet, so please keep the comments to yourselves. Next is Paul Bunyan.

Paul: Now, I don't like to boast, and I don't like certain folks calling my Babe a stinky cow. Babe is a blue ox, and the strongest and hardest-working animal there is, next to me. When I was born, it took five storks, working overtime, to carry me to my parents.

Bill: I thought you might have started out as some kind of foot ailment.

Paul: Huh. Wisconsin used to have so many trees, they were as thick as the hair on a dog's tail. They were so thick it was like all of Wisconsin was one forest, one tree, in fact. And with one mighty swing of my ax, I cleared acres and acres of trees.

John: Ho-hum.

Paul: And all those trees fell in the Wisconsin River, and there were so many trees they turned that river into a logjam so solid you could build a house in the middle and not even know there was water underneath. So I sent Babe into the river ahead of the jam and started peppering that fine ox with buckshot. And he thought some kind of big fly was pestering him, so he switched his tail this way and that, stirring up the water into a whirlpool so fierce that logjam broke apart like it was made of twigs. After that, Babe and I were both a little tired, so I dug a little water hole for Babe to drink out of, and the people around that hole started to call it Lake Michigan, and it is still there today.

Bill: What a snooze.

Paul: You can do better?

Bill: I sure hope so.

Referee: Enough. Next is John Henry.

John: Some of you may not know me, but I was a steel-driving man, black as the rock I blasted with my hammer, and the strongest and fastest man that ever worked the rails. I could work that hammer and drill faster than any man— machine, too. My hammer was like greased lightning, and many a holder lost his hand for failing to move it fast enough. We took to drilling a tunnel through Big Bend Mountain, over a mile of solid rock. Me and my hammer and star drill could clear 15 feet a day. My reputation traveled far and wide, and one day this little man with a shiny contraption showed up in camp and challenged me to a contest. I told that little man, "Mister, you can't even pick up a sledge," and he said, "Not me. I want you to challenge my steam machine. It's the fastest drilling thing you ever saw." And I laughed so hard, the folks in the next county looked to the sky thinking a storm was brewing.

Bill: Must have been that tornado I rode.

John: So the contest began, and the tunnel was filled with smoke and dust, that machine clanking away—and doing a mighty fine job, I might add—but I was slinging two 20-pound hammers like they were made of air. And we hammered and banged, banged and hammered, for 35 minutes unending. And at the finish, when the dust cleared, that machine had drilled a nine-foot hole, and the men stopped cheering and a great hush fell on the place because they thought I had failed. But then they added up my two holes— a total of 14 feet—and sure enough, I had won. But I was so dead-tired I fell to the ground and hit so hard some folks thought an earthquake had struck. Even the mighty Mississipp was knocked off course.

Paul: I heard you died from that contest.

John: That, sir, is just a tall tale—just exaggeration. Here I am, can't you see?

Referee: Next we have Coyote.

Coyote: Hey, Bill, remember that time you helped me make the Grand Canyon?

Bill: I recollect the event, but I don't rightly recall you being there.

Paul: That's because neither one of you was there. I dug out the Grand Canyon.

Coyote: Oh, you're right. I was just kidding. I was thinking about the Columbia River, not the Colorado. My people were once great and many, and we were one with the Earth. When we asked it for help, it came to our aid. I was walking one day—a very hot day—and I felt like some shade. So I asked my father, Great Sky, for a cloud, and a cloud came to shade me. But it was still very hot, and the one cloud was not good enough for me. So I asked the sky for more clouds, and more clouds came. But it was still hot, and my brother, the ground, was very thirsty, so I asked the sky for rain, and a light rain began to fall. More rain, I asked of my father, the sky, and the rain fell harder and harder until it was a downpour. I asked for a creek to cool my feet, and a creek sprang up beside me. I asked that it be deeper, and the creek became a roaring river. I suppose I asked for too much—we must be careful what we ask for—and the water caught me and pulled me along, tossing me on its mighty back, playing with me for being so greedy. At last, nearly drowned, I was thrown on the shore, and the river rushed on its way. I was very weak, and I fell into a deep sleep. When I awoke, my cousins, the buzzards, were staring in my face, seeing if I was dead. But I yelled at them, "I am not dead yet!" And I told them my friend, the river, would get them too, so they flew away in fear. And that is how the Columbia River began.

Referee: All right, then. For our last liar, I mean storyteller, tonight, we have Pecos Bill.

Bill: Thanks. Well, I'm so famous and well known that you have probably heard every story I might tell.

Sue: Just get on with it, Bill. We have business to finish.

Bill: Uh, yeah. OK, well, then, when I was a young sprout, knee high to a grasshopper, I was riding with my family in the wagon. Now, there was oodles of kids, so many my folks could barely keep them straight, and as we crossed through a washout, I fell out of the wagon. Well, I hollered, but there was so much noise they didn't hear me, and I got left behind. Well, I wandered around a bit, but since I was only three days old, there wasn't much I could do for myself. As luck would have it, a pack of coyotes came by about that time and took me in.

Coyote: I have never forgiven my brothers for that.

Bill: Well, anyway, to make a long story longer, they made me an honorary coyote and raised me as one of their own. I was a good coyote too, harder than nails and tougher than whip leather. When it came time for me to leave, they set me toward the west, and before I knew it I was a cowboy down in Texas. I didn't know much about riding, so I caught me a mountain lion, saddled it up, and rode it for a good long spell. During that time I invented the lasso and taught broncos to buck and cowboys to ride them. As you all know, never was a horse that could throw me, except Widowmaker came close once or twice. And the only time I did get throwed off was by a tornado in Kansas. I had done about all I could do in Texas, so I headed north for a little trip, sightseeing, you might say. Before long I found myself in Kansas and when I looked up, the sky had turned dark as night and the wind was howling and whooshing like the end of the world.

Paul: That was Babe bellowing.

John: That was me snoring.

Jane: That was me moaning when Wild Bill passed.

Sally: That was my cousin. I sent him to whup you.

Bill: Excuse me? I believe it is my turn. You all had your turns. It's not my fault you all are so dull.

(He clears his throat to continue.)

Bill: No, it was just a tornado. Like I said, the sky was dark as night, all black and green and oily, and the wind was roaring so loud people in Californee woke up from the racket. Well, I like peace and quiet myself, so I yelled at the top of my lungs, "Yeehaw!" And that old tornado paid me no mind, and I yelled again, even louder, "Yeehaw!" And it just kept on going on its merry way, purty as you please. Now, if there's one thing I can't stand, it's being ignored, so I caught that there tornado by the tail and then I . . . *(He pauses.)*

All: Yes . . .

Bill: Well, then I . . .

All: Yessss . . .

Bill: Well, then I just hopped aboard and held on like glue. That mean old tornado didn't like that at all, so it danced this way to Nebraskee and then it ran that way to Missouri, and then it turned upside down so the stars were where the ground should be. And all that time I'm holding on like there was no tomorrow. But that tornado, it was a smart one, and it raced out into the desert, where it must have been 150 degrees if it was any. And my hands got all slick and slippery, and I knew I was losing my grip, and before I could say "jackrabbit," that tornado tossed me a mile into the air. And I started falling, and I fell, and I fell, and I fell some more, thinking sure as thunder this was the end of me. And then I hit the ground so hard it knocked a hole way below sea level. Well, I got up and dusted the sand off my jeans and headed back to Texas. And I hear tell, people started calling that place Death Valley. All I know is, it was almost the death of me.

Paul: I don't believe that.

Bill: Oh, and we're supposed to believe you chopped down Wisconsin with one swing.

Paul: It's true.

Referee: Enough! Enough!

End of Round Three

Round Four

Announcer: Spirits are high here, ladies and gentlemen, and the votes have been counted. Let's go to the referee for the final count.

Referee: Well, we have a most interesting situation here. It seems we have a seven-way tie.

Paul: What?

John: That can't be!

Bill: That's the goll-darndest thing I ever heard!

Sally: I knew I should have whupped you all when I had the chance.

Sue: Aw, I could whup you with my eyes closed.

Coyote: I could get my cousins, the buzzards, to whup you all.

Paul: Babe could whup you with his tail.

Bill: I could whup you all with Widowmaker strapped on my back.

John: Aw, you couldn't whup your way out of a paper sack.

All: *(Except Jane)* Grrr!

Jane: Wait, wait. Whupping doesn't ever solve a problem for long. Soon as you turn around, somebody else shows up to whup you. That's what happened to Wild Bill.

All: Rest his soul.

Jane: Now, I suggest you all sit down and get a big old cup of sassafras tea. We can chew over these matters further.

All: Well, OK.

John: Well, come sit down with us, Jane.

Jane: No, thanks. I think I'll stand.

End of Play

Showdown at the Not-So-OK Corral: What Do You Remember?

Darken the letter by the correct answer.

1. What kind of work does John Henry do?
   Ⓐ lumberjack
   Ⓑ cowboy
   Ⓒ wagon driver
   Ⓓ railroad worker

2. When does Coyote tell his story?
   Ⓐ before Calamity Jane tells hers
   Ⓑ before Paul Bunyan tells his
   Ⓒ before Pecos Bill tells his
   Ⓓ after Pecos Bill tells his

3. Slue-Foot Sue says she has to spin a yarn. What is a *yarn?*
   Ⓐ thread
   Ⓑ tall tale
   Ⓒ shirt
   Ⓓ jacket

4. The play is mostly about
   Ⓐ the adventures of some unusual characters.
   Ⓑ how to catch big fish.
   Ⓒ how to have fun with weather.
   Ⓓ how to drill a hole.

5. You can conclude that
   Ⓐ all the characters wanted to win the showdown.
   Ⓑ all the characters wanted to lose the showdown.
   Ⓒ the characters did not care about winning or losing.
   Ⓓ the characters did not like to tell stories.

6. If Pecos Bill gets another chance to ride a tornado, he will probably
   Ⓐ get a raincoat.
   Ⓑ tell Sally Ann to stop sending tornadoes.
   Ⓒ not ride it.
   Ⓓ start chopping down trees.

7. At the end of the play, Calamity Jane says, "Whupping doesn't ever solve a problem for long. Soon as you turn around, somebody else shows up to whup you." What does she mean?

   _____

   _____

Showdown at the Not-So-OK Corral: What's That Word?

⭐ **Darken the circle by the vocabulary word that best completes each sentence.**

1. Someone who competes in a game is
   a _____.
   - Ⓐ penalty
   - Ⓑ contestant
   - Ⓒ contraption
   - Ⓓ plague

2. To remember something is to recall
   or _____ it.
   - Ⓐ plague
   - Ⓑ prefer
   - Ⓒ recollect
   - Ⓓ buzzard

3. Things that people have done for a
   long time are called _____.
   - Ⓐ traditions
   - Ⓑ participants
   - Ⓒ galluses
   - Ⓓ contestants

4. A person who does something
   wrong is given a _____.
   - Ⓐ contraption
   - Ⓑ penalty
   - Ⓒ ornery
   - Ⓓ honorary

5. Another name for a machine is a
   _____.
   - Ⓐ contestant
   - Ⓑ tradition
   - Ⓒ buzzard
   - Ⓓ contraption

6. To choose one thing instead of
   another is to _____ it.
   - Ⓐ prefer
   - Ⓑ plague
   - Ⓒ recall
   - Ⓓ penalty

7. A person who is hard to get along
   with is _____.
   - Ⓐ abiding
   - Ⓑ honorary
   - Ⓒ ornery
   - Ⓓ floundering

8. Something that is splashing or
   thrashing about is _____.
   - Ⓐ abiding
   - Ⓑ floundering
   - Ⓒ honorary
   - Ⓓ galluses

9. A bird that eats dead animals is a
   _____.
   - Ⓐ plague
   - Ⓑ contraption
   - Ⓒ tradition
   - Ⓓ buzzard

10. A very serious outbreak of disease is
    called a _____.
    - Ⓐ buzzard
    - Ⓑ plague
    - Ⓒ participant
    - Ⓓ penalty

Showdown at the Not-So-OK Corral: **What Do You Think?**

Many of the characters in the play use incorrect grammar. Read each incorrect sentence. Then, rewrite the sentence using correct grammar.

1. Sue, sweetheart, I ain't seen you in a month of Sundays.

_____

2. And purty soon, there wasn't nothing I could do.

_____

3. The next day we was married.

_____

4. I been bouncing around ever since.

_____

5. The only time I did get throwed off was by a tornado in Kansas.

_____

_____

Showdown at the Not-So-OK Corral: **Write Away!**

Write your own tall tale and read it to the class. Before you begin, remember that the key feature of a tall tale is exaggeration. When writers exaggerate, they overstate or magnify something. Often they use similes and metaphors. Practice writing exaggerated versions of the following sentences. The examples are based on the play.

Statement of Fact	*Exaggeration*
I was a strong woman.	I was a big old gal who could do the work of ten men—easy.
The wind blew hard.	The wind howled and whooshed like the end of the world.
The temperature today is 105° F.	_____
My parents are mad about my grades.	_____
The roads through the jungle were hard to travel.	_____

Studying the Elements of a Play

A play is a story that is acted out. Every play has characters, a setting, and a plot. Complete each of the following statements about the play you just read.

Title of the play: _____

Characters are the people or animals in the play.

1. The most important character* in the play is _____

2. Two minor, or less important, characters are _____ and

_____

Setting tells when and where the events in the play take place.

3. The time (past, present, future) the events in the play take place is _____

_____

4. The place where the events take place is _____

_____

Plot is the story the play tells. Plot includes the problem that the main character faces; the main events, or attempts by the main character to solve the problem; and the play's ending.

5. The problem that the main character faces is _____

_____

_____

6. Two important events, or attempts to solve the problem, are _____

_____

_____

7. The play ends when _____

_____

Some plays have more than one main character.

Comparing Characters

When you think about how characters are alike or different, you compare them. Use the chart below to compare two characters in the play. Place the character's initials in the boxes that best describe him or her. You may add more characteristics to the chart.

Play: _____

Character: _____

Character: _____

	VERY	SOMEWHAT	NEITHER	SOMEWHAT	VERY	
good						evil
happy						unhappy
careful						clumsy
lucky						unlucky
wise						foolish
friendly						unfriendly
kind						unkind
honest						dishonest
gentle						rough
brave						afraid
proud						ashamed
successful						unsuccessful

✏️ Write Away!

Use a separate sheet of paper to write two or more paragraphs comparing the two characters. Explain how they are alike and how they are different.

Understanding the Characters

The characters in a play do and say things that show what kind of people they are. Select three of the most important characters in the play. Answer the questions about each character you have chosen.

Title of the play: _____

1. Character: _____

What kind of person is this character? _____

_____

_____

Give an example of something the character did or said in the play that supports the description you have given. _____

_____

_____

2. Character: _____

What kind of person is this character? _____

_____

_____

Give an example of something the character did or said in the play that supports the description you have given. _____

_____

_____

3. Character: _____

What kind of person is this character? _____

_____

_____

Give an example of something the character did or said in the play that supports the description you have given. _____

_____

_____

Name ______________________ Date ______________

Making a Play Map

Use the play map shown here to tell what happens in the play.

Play Title: ______________________

Characters: ______________________

____

Setting: ______________________

____

Problem: ______________________

____

Main Event:

Main Event:

Main Event:

Main Event:

Solution:

Choosing an Alternate Ending

Unless a play is a historical drama, the author chooses how the play ends. Analyze the ending of the play you have just read by answering questions 1–5. Then create a different ending.

Title of the play: _____

1. Describe the problem that the main character* faces in the play.

_____

_____

2. What choices does the main character have for solving the problem?

_____

_____

3. How does the main character choose to solve the problem?

_____

_____

4. Do you think the main character makes the right choice? Explain your answer.

_____

_____

_____

5. If you were in the main character's place, what choice would you make?

_____

_____

6. Imagine that the main character makes a different choice. Then, write a new ending for the play. Use a separate sheet of paper if you need more space.

_____

_____

_____

_____

_____

*Some plays have more than one main character.

Changed

by Henry Wadsworth Longfellow

Group 1: From the outskirts of the town
Where of old the mile-stone stood,

Group 2: Now a stranger, looking down
I behold the shadowy crown

All: Of the dark and haunted wood.

Solo 1: Is it changed, or am I changed?

Group 1: Ah! the oaks are fresh and green,
But the friends with whom I ranged

Group 2: Through their thickets are estranged
By the years that intervene.

Group 1: Bright as ever flows the sea,
Bright as ever shines the Sun,

Solo 2: But alas! they seem to me

Group 2: Not the Sun that used to be,
Not the tides that used to run.

The Lamplighter
by Robert Louis Stevenson

Solo 1:   My tea is nearly ready and the sun has left the sky.

Solo 2:   It's time to take the window to see Leerie
going by;

Solo 3:   For every night at teatime and before you take
your seat,

All: With lantern and with ladder he comes posting up
the street.

Solo 4:   Now Tom would be a driver and Maria go to sea,

Solo 5:   And my papa is a banker and as rich as he can be;

Solo 6:   But I, when I am stronger and can choose what
I'm to do,

All: Leerie, I'll go 'round at night and light the lamps
with you!

Solo 7:   For we are very lucky, with a lamp before the
door,

Solo 8:   And Leerie stops to light it as he lights so many
more;

Solo 9:   And oh! before you hurry by with ladder and with
light;

All: Leerie, see a little child and nod to him tonight!

Eldorado

by Edgar Allan Poe

Group 1: Gaily bedight,
A gallant knight
In sunshine and in shadow,

Group 2: Had journeyed long,
Singing a song,

Solo 1: In search of Eldorado.

Group 1: But he grew old—
This knight so bold—

Group 2: And o'er his heart a shadow
Fell, as he found
No spot of ground

Solo 2: That looked like Eldorado.

Group 1: And, as his strength
Failed him at length
He met a pilgrim shadow—

Solo 3: "Shadow," said he,
"Where can it be—
This land of Eldorado?"

Group 2: "Over the Mountains
Of the Moon,
Down the Valley of the Shadow,

Solo 4: Ride, boldly ride,"
The shade replied,
"If you seek for Eldorado!"

Invictus
by William Ernest Henley

Group 1:   Out of the night that covers me,
Black as the Pit from pole to pole,

Solo 1:   I thank whatever gods may be
For my unconquerable soul.

Group 2:   In the fell clutch of circumstance

Solo 2:   I have not winced nor cried aloud.

Group 2:   Under the bludgeonings of chance

Solo 3:   My head is bloody, but unbowed.

Group 1:   Beyond this place of wrath and tears
Looms but the horror of the shade,

Group 2:   And yet the menace of the years
Finds, and shall find, me unafraid.

Solo 4:   It matters not how strait the gate,
How charged with punishments the scroll,

All: I am the master of my fate:
I am the captain of my soul.

Three Wise Women

by Elizabeth T. Corbett

Group 1: Three wise old women were they, were they,
Who went to walk on a winter day:

Solo 1: One carried a basket to hold some berries,

Solo 2: One carried a ladder to climb for cherries,

Group 2: The third, and she was the wisest one,
Carried a fan to keep off the Sun.

All: But they went so far, and they went so fast,
They quite forgot their way at last,
So one of the wise women cried in a fright,

Solo 3: "Suppose we should meet a bear tonight!
Suppose he should eat me!"

Solo 4: "And me!"

Solo 5: "And me!!!"

All: "What is to be done?" cried all the three.

Group 1: "Dear, dear!" said one, "We'll climb a tree,
There out of the way of the bears we'll be."

Three Wise Women, p. 2

Group 2:   But there wasn't a tree for miles around;
They were too frightened to stay on the ground,
So they climbed their ladder up to the top,
And sat there screaming,

All: "We'll drop! We'll drop!"

Group 1:   But the wind was strong as wind could be,
And blew their ladder right out to sea;
So the three wise women were all afloat
In a leaky ladder instead of a boat,

Group 2:   And every time the waves rolled in,
Of course the poor things were wet to the skin.
Then they took their basket, the water to bail,
They put up their fan instead of a sail:

Solo 6:   But what became of the wise women then,
Whether they ever sailed home again,
Whether they saw any bears, or no.
You must find out, for I don't know.

Answer Key

page 26

1. C, **2.** C, **3.** B, **4.** D, **5.** C, **6.** B,
7. Tommy says that lots of people like his grandmother and Mr. Tuttle never learned to read, and they are too ashamed to admit it. So, they let other people read for them.

page 27

Across: 5. awesome, **6.** supervising, **7.** admit, **8.** literacy

Down: 1. absolute, **2.** exasperation, **3.** scowls, **4.** elementary

page 28

Posters will vary. Check to see how students have conveyed the message without using words.

Write Away: Thank-you notes will vary but should be based on the play and contain adequate detail.

page 42

1. A, **2.** C, **3.** B, **4.** B, **5.** A, **6.** D,
7. Answers will vary but should suggest that Jimmy is a good fellow at heart, as the warden noted. His love for Annabel and her family overrides selfish considerations.

page 43

1. B, **2.** D, **3.** A, **4.** C, **5.** D, **6.** A, **7.** B, **8.** D, **9.** B, **10.** C

page 44

Reasons will vary but might include pardons for good behavior and no pardons to keep criminals from repeating crimes.

Write Away: Paragraphs will vary but should be based on reasons given in the chart.

page 66

1. C, **2.** B, **3.** D, **4.** A, **5.** D, **6.** C,
7. Jane made a birdhouse for her stepfather and a tie rack for her real father. One can assume that she has a positive relationship with both men.

page 67

1. brackets, **2.** thumbs up, **3.** elbow grease, **4.** nativity, **5.** split up, **6.** project, **7.** glares, **8.** clam up, **9.** positive, **10.** figured

page 68

Decorations will vary.

Write Away: Acts will vary but should be based on the play, feature Kevin's family as characters, and convey both action and emotions.

page 90

1. C, **2.** C, **3.** B, **4.** A, **5.** B, **6.** A,
7. Qualities will vary but include friendly, forgiving, understanding, compassionate, determined.

page 91

1. The noise around the swimming pool was deafening.

2. Juan was lucky he did not lose his leg altogether.

3. Juan was frozen momentarily on the starting block.

4. Juan did not know about Annie's disability.

5. Life is tough for Juan.

6. Juan spoke bitterly about his hurt leg.

7. Juan did not like Annie's sharp words.

8. Juan turned abruptly and headed for the locker room.

Answer Key, p. 2

page 92

Safety posters will vary but should have good safety tips.

Write Away: Essays will vary but should be closely based on a character in the play.

page 112

1. D, **2.** B, **3.** A, **4.** C, **5.** D, **6.** B, **7.** Like Lance, Alex believes that people expect him to be something he is not really.

page 113

1. consumer, **2.** guidance, **3.** fashion, **4.** criticize, **5.** concert, **6.** deranged, **7.** melodious, **8.** Vocal, **9.** security, **10.** concession, **11.** autograph, **12.** regret, **13.** crazy, sane, **14.** valuable, worthless, **15.** buyer, seller, **16.** pleasant, unpleasant

page 114

1. $160; **2.** $110,000; **3.** $16,500; **4.** $2,559.25; **5.** $142.55

Write Away: Paragraphs will vary but should include the writer's expectations and feelings.

page 136

1. C, **2.** B, **3.** A, **4.** D, **5.** B, **6.** C, **7.** Answers will vary but should suggest that making bad use of science can lead to confusion or dangerous situations.

page 137

Across: 1. chaos, **5.** mission, **8.** trespassing, **9.** illegal

Down: 2. original, **3.** caution, **4.** unleash, **6.** normal, **7.** insane

page 138

Lists of qualities and traits will vary. Plays will vary.

Write Away: Paragraphs will vary but should include reasonable points supporting the side chosen.

page 161

1. D, **2.** C, **3.** B, **4.** A, **5.** A, **6.** C, **7.** Jane's point is that violence doesn't really solve problems; if anything, violence causes more violence.

page 162

1. B, **2.** C, **3.** A, **4.** B, **5.** D, **6.** A, **7.** C, **8.** B, **9.** D, **10.** B

page 163

Sentences may vary.

1. Sue, sweetheart, I haven't seen you in a month of Sundays.

2. And fairly soon, there wasn't anything I could do.

3. The next day we were married.

4. I have been bouncing around ever since.

5. The only time I did get thrown off was by a tornado in Kansas.

Write Away: Tall tales will vary but should contain exaggeration. Sentence revisions will vary.